C·L·A·S·S·I·C
Ferrari

CLB 2696
© Colour Library Books Ltd., Godalming, Surrey, England.
This 1991 edition published by Crescent Books,
distributed by Outlet Book Company, Inc., a Random House Company,
225 Park Avenue South, New York, New York 10003.
Printed and bound in Italy
All rights reserved.
ISBN 0 517 06580 0
8 7 6 5 4 3 2 1

C·L·A·S·S·I·C
Ferrari

CRESCENT BOOKS
NEW YORK

FOREWORD

Ferrari is the greatest name in the history of Grand Prix motor racing, and one of the greatest names in the history of the automobile. Therefore, as an ex-Ferrari driver, as well as a car enthusiast, it gives me great pleasure to write this foreword to Godfrey Eaton's well researched and superbly illustrated book on Ferrari.

During the time I was a member of the Ferrari team I got to know Enzo Ferrari extremely well. The Old Man is not only a personality, but also a good and kindly man who lives up to his great reputation. In all my years with Ferrari, I never had a single problem with him on a one-to-one basis. Any problems there were always emanated from his advisors, who were so much in awe of this monumental patriarch. They were the source of any misunderstandings and bad decisions that were taken.

Ferrari, the racing team, is unique in the world; a combination of incredible resources, up-to-date testing facilities and brilliant engineers. In 1975, the Ferrari 312T was simply years ahead of its rivals. Out of eleven races I started nine times in pole position and won five times, with almost twenty points lead in the World Championship. Ferrari that year changed the face of Grand Prix Racing and provided an example of technical development and precision workmanship that had never before existed in motor racing.

Ferrari, the road cars, have long epitomized the very best in grand touring cars, and it is therefore no surprise to find that Ferrari sports cars, particularly the twelve cylinder models, have pride of place in many of the more important collections throughout the world.

Niki Lauda

Preceding page: Didier Pironi in the new 126C2 V6 formula 1 turbo car
during the 1982 South African GP. He completed 71 of the 77 lap race finishing in 18th
place. Chassis No. 056. Left: Two views of David Piper's 1965 365P2/3 chassis No.
0836. Piper was, in the main, a privateer driving Ferrari sports racing cars with reasonable
success in the long distance races such as the Daytona 24-hour, Sebring and Reims
12-hour, Montlhery 1000 km etc. This car is still raced on occasions.

EARLY AMBITION

History shows us that there are few young men who set out early in life with one or more ambitions and finally settle on one which they then pursue with a determination and single mindedness of purpose to achieve their goal. The young Enzo Ferrari had three ambitions; to become an opera singer which was not possible as he had no ear for music; to become a sporting journalist which he never achieved although he was, in later life, a good public relations man for his own concern, and his final choice was to be a racing driver and connected with the automobile industry. It was as well for all those who not only follow the sport of motor racing, but who also love beautiful and exotic cars that he chose the third option, for Enzo Ferrari is one of those rare persons who have become a legend in their lifetime.

An Italian, he was born on 18th February 1898 on the outskirts of Modena, in the province Emilia-Romagna, where his father had a metal workshop which was obviously prosperous for he owned a motor car, a mode of transport available only to those with a reasonable income. Foreseeing the future of the automobile, a motor repair shop was added

1

2

3

6

to the business. It was here that Enzo Ferrari learnt the basic mechanical skills, although his father would have preferred that he studied automobile engineering at the local technical college. It was only in later years that he probably regretted not heeding the advice, but this was no hindrance to him in his chosen career as an administrator, for he was an opportunist who always selected and got under contract the man he needed for any particular project.

Enzo's desire to become a racing driver was probably influenced, at least partly, by his father who would take him along to all race meetings held in the locality and like all schoolboys he, no doubt, dreamt of emulating the feats of such great drivers of the 'heroic age' as Vincenzo Lancia and Felice Nazzaro. However, the First World War broke out before he had reached manhood and when old enough he was recruited into the forces, where he found life far from satisfactory and highly distasteful. He was depressed and his health suffered, so he was more than pleased when invalided out of the army at the end of hostilities.

With a letter of introduction in his pocket he went along to FIAT hoping for a job, only to be told they had no use for his services. Before long, however, he found employment as a tester for a firm which bought up Lancia light truck chassis and rebodied them as passenger cars. His work frequently took him to Milan and on one trip he met Ugo Sivocci, who tested cars for Costruzioni Meccaniche Nazionali. This company was also in the business of reconstructing cars, but from parts which were sold off from the Isotta Fraschini factory, and since they would be building a car or two for racing Enzo decided he would join Sivocci. In 1919 he had his opportunity and finished a creditable fourth at the Parma Reggio de Berceto hill climb. On 23rd November in the same year he and Sivocci entered the Tenth 'Targa Florio' race over the Medium Madonie Circuit in Sicily with their CMNs, and after 268½ miles (four laps) over this most gruelling road circuit in the world, Sivocci finished in seventh place, but Ferrari was unplaced, having exceeded the time stipulated. He had been delayed in one of the villages on the route, where a meeting was being held!

The following year he joined the Milanese firm of Alfa Romeo as a

(1) Without doubt, the GTO cars are those most sought after by Ferrarists and during the period 1961 to 1963 scored many racing successes. (2) Whilst it was never a popular model due to its rather ordinary looks, the 330GT 2+2 V12 4-litre was nonetheless a reliable and very fast grand touring car. (3) One of the short-lived line of four-cylinder sports racing cars, the 1954 860 Monza was a brute to drive and although it wasn't a complete success, it was by no means a failure. (4) A Giovanni Michelotti designed Vignale body on a 1950 195S chassis. (5) A very early car. The cycle-winged 166 Spider Corsa was used in this form for sports racing but with wings removed for grand prix events. (6) A single carburettor Type 166 road car with coachwork by Carrozzeria Touring (circa 1948).

works' driver and Sivocci followed him; this was an upward step in the automobile world especially as their team mates, Giuseppe Campari and Antonio Ascari, were already famous racing drivers. He celebrated his good fortune by taking second place in the Eleventh Targa Florio and the following year he was fifth. 1922 was the last year he contested the race but he finished down the field in 16th position. While he was to compete in Alfa Romeos until 1931, the management at Milan had noted his potential as an administrator and he became an office bound executive. As the company were at that time looking for prestige in the world of motor racing, and this meant grand prix racing, a department at the works was being built up towards this end, but it lacked the necessary technicians. In 1922 FIAT had carried all before them on the grand prix scene with their six cylinder two litre 804, which had been designed by Vittorio Jano. Enzo Ferrari, deciding he needed his expertise, persuaded him to leave the FIAT organisation and join Alfa Romeo and at the same time he persuaded Luigi Bazzi, who was to become one of the world's foremost automobile technicians, to do the same. Ferrari and Bazzi were to remain friends and partners for the rest of their working lives.

In the space of a few months Jano's design for his new masters, the straight eight supercharged two litre Alfa Romeo P2, was ready and on

1

2

(1) The compact 4.4 litre engine of the Lampredi designed twin overhead camshaft six cylinder in line 121LM. (2) Based on the Colombo designed V12 engine, the mid-engined 250LM was highly successful in competition whether raced by the factory or in the hands of privateers. (3) The 121LM was not one of Ferrari's best sports racing cars. It had been developed from the not too successful four cylinder 625 racing cars, with two cylinders added. It was sometimes referred to as a Super Monza. (4) One of Ferrari's successful GT racing cars, the long wheel base

3

250GT berlinetta, called the Tour de France, is much prized. It was in production from 1955 to 1959 with some 84 examples made. The car shown is a 1958 model. (5) This particular 250GTO has probably had more words written about it than any other Ferrari. The owner is Nick Mason, who has a number of other highly desirable Ferraris and other exotic cars.

4

5

SCUDERIA FERRARI

3rd August 1924 in its first Grand Prix (the French) at Lyons, Giuseppe Campari took first place, followed home by two Delages and in fourth position Louis Wagner's P2. Ferrari was due to drive but felt unwell, he did however have the satisfaction of proving he was qualified to select the right man for a particular project.

In 1929 Ferrari took a further step towards fulfilling his ambition to be his 'own man' when he left Alfa Romeo, on amicable terms, to set up a racing establishment, the Societa Anonima Scuderia Ferrari. At that time the Milanese firm had financial problems and had to curtail their racing activities, but were willing to hand over their cars to Ferrari, who would prepare and race them. On the other hand Ferrari's immediate financial problems were solved when he met two young and wealthy Alfa Romeo amateur drivers at an official dinner. On outlining his future plans the two, Caniato and Tadini, agreed to put up the necessary working capital, and on 1st December the Scuderia was officially formed. Further contact between Alfa Romeo's management and Ferrari had secured an agency to sell and service their cars in the Emilia-Romagna and Marche provinces; he also obtained financial assistance and products from Pirelli, Shell and Bosch.

Success was hard to come by, as the Scuderia were trying to match their sports 1750 Alfas against the much faster racing Maseratis and Bugattis. It was not until Ferrari was loaned an up-dated P2 that the Scuderia had its first success, when Tazio Nuvolari made fastest time of the day, and also broke the record, for the Trieste-Opicina hill climb on 15th June 1930. In 1931 he was entrusted with a team of 2300 Monza Alfas for the annual Mille Miglia race and was rewarded by Campari taking the chequered flag with Nuvolari in third place, but these cars did not bring him the race successes he was looking for.

By 1932 Vittorio Jano had come up with a successor to the P2, the

(1) There is no doubt that the front-
engined V12 four camshaft 275GTB/4
was one of the most handsome road cars
produced by Ferrari. 350 models came from
the factory between 1966 and 1968. (2)
This short wheelbase 250GT berlinetta
had coachwork by Drogo, making a
change in styling which gives the car a
squarish but pleasantly rakish look. (3)
The styling on the 1956 410 Superamerica
shows the mid-fifties American influence

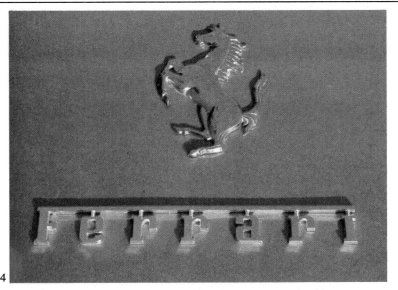

4

when preposterous fins were all the rage in
the States. (4) Tail-piece on the boot of a
330GTC of the prancing horse logo and
also the correct 'Ferrari' lettering logo. (5)
One of only three 250LMBs built. Body
style was similar to the 330LMB but on a
shorter chassis. (6) The 330GTC
passenger car had a factory run of 600,
built between 1966 and 1968. (7) Picture
shows the grille of the 250 LMB. (8)
Another shot of the elegant 330GTC.

5

6

7

8

Type B Monoposto (known as the P3). After a successful first season in the hands of the Scuderia, the Alfa Romeo company withdrew the cars and Ferrari was, once more, left with the out-dated Monza two-seaters. In an effort to extract more power, he increased the original capacity from 2300 to 2600 cc, but in so doing the cars became less reliable. Somewhat disenchanted with the cars, Ferrari sought some solace by turning his attention to motor cycle racing, always popular in Italy. Collecting a team of British Rudge and Norton two-wheelers, he proceeded over a three year period, to win National Championships in the 250, 350 and 500 cc classes. While this was going on Pirelli, the tyre manufacturers, decided they were losing valuable publicity while the P3 cars were inactive. In 1934, therefore, they forced Alfa Romeo management to turn the cars over to Ferrari and at the same time release Luigi Bazzi and Attilo Marinoni to look after and prepare them for racing. Unfortunately the Scuderia had lost a years' racing successes, for by 1934 the German firms of Mercedes-Benz and Auto Union had appeared on the racing scene with huge financial backing from the Reich Government. Independent firms such as Alfa Romeo, were left at a disadvantage with little cash to produce new cars or make the necessary modifications to up-date existing ones. Despite this, the Milanese firm was still designing and producing a few racing cars with which the Scuderia mainly contested the less prestigious events, but overall it was a quiet period which did not suit Ferrari.

By 1935 both Bazzi and Ferrari were somewhat desperate, so between them they agreed on a project which Bazzi termed 'a youthful

1

2

3

folly'. Using Alfa Romeo parts they built two cars; each car had two eight-in-line engines, one placed in the normal position at the front and the second behind the driver: they were called Bi-Motores. On speed and reliability they were more than a challenge to the German teams, in fact they were too fast for any racing tyres which had been produced up to that time, so that what the cars gained on speed over their rivals, they lost due to the number of pit stops made to change tyres.

The formula for Grand Prix cars was to be changed in 1938 with a bewildering number of capacities depending on whether supercharged or normally aspirated engines were used. With the new regulations Alfa Romeo laid down a programme for three cars and decided to race them under a new organisation to be called Alfa Corse, with Ferrari in command.

Apart from the premier grade of racing, voiturette racing was gaining in popularity, this was for cars with a maximum capacity of 1500 cc and was contested mainly by the British E.R.As and Italian 4C and 6C Maseratis. These cars appealed to Ferrari and in 1937 Alfa Romeo allowed him to build a batch of four and loaned Gioacchino Colombo to head a design team. The Alfetta 158, as they were named, had an eight-in-line engine and the intial bench tests gave a respectable 190 bhp at 6500 rpm. A highly successful design, it won more than its share of events but suffered one devastating defeat at Tripoli in 1939, when Ferrari was anticipating a resounding victory. Unbeknown to the Italians, the Mercedes Factory has built and entered a team of 1½ litre V8 cars designated the W165. They annihilated the Alfettas, returned to Germany and never raced again.

Pictures (1, 2 and 3) show one of the most sleek and handsome sports racing cars to come from the Ferrari factory: the 206SP. Its ancestry can be dated back to Vittorio Jano's design of the 65 degree four cam V6 F2 of 1956 and designated 156F2. The history of the various SP cars (sports prototype) is baffling. Some 15 206SPs were built but racing successes were hard to come by. The car shown is a complete rebuild by Dudley Mason-Styrron. It has been a very successful hill climb car and has taken many concours awards. The 206SP was the forerunner of the transversely mounted rear-engined 206GT road car from which was derived the sensual looking Dino 246 in GT and Spider form. All coachwork was designed by the master craftsmen at Pininfarina. The Dino 246 was in production from 1969 to

4

1974 and was replaced by the 308GTB (also in Spider form), considered by many as the greatest design with its curvaceous, flowing lines all derived from the original 206SP coachwork. It serves to show that a sound basic design can be carried forward for a number of years without losing its place in the exotic car market. Pictures (4 & 5) are of Don Nelson's 250GTO which is always turned out in immaculate style. Some 15 of these cars are to be found in the UK, from a total production of 39.

5

The Alfettas went through several stages of modification, appearing as the 158C in 1940 and 158D in 1942 and its final development as the 159. It reigned supreme in post war (1940-1945) Grand Prix racing until 1952, when it was obvious that the larger capacity unsupercharged cars of Ferrari (who was now designing and building cars under his own name), would have the beating of it unless Alfa Romeo carried out extensive and costly modifications. So finally Ferrari with his own cars had the better of a car, originally designed and built by him in 1937, the up-dated Alfetta 158.

But to go back. 1938 was another turning point in Enzo Ferrari's career and a significant step nearer to his ultimate ambition. As previously related he had been appointed team manager of Alfa Corse but found the change from being his own master somewhat irksome. To

add to his difficulties he was unable to work side by side with Alfa Romeo's Spanish engineer, Wilfredo Ricart, whom he found obnoxious. He resigned, as did his friend Luigi Bazzi, Alberto Massimino and one or two other technicians, and they all returned to Modena. Thus, after 18 years of working for and with the Milanese company, he finally severed all ties and under the separation agreement was not allowed to build any cars bearing his name for four years.

Ferrari kept to the agreed terms but in 1940 he built two sports racing cars from FIAT components for the annual Mille Miglia race: they had a cubic capacity of 1500 cc. The name on the radiator shell said Vettura 815 and one of the cars still exists in a museum. Incidentally neither car finished the race.

After the 1940-1945 war Ferrari was soon back in business at

A DREAM REALISED

1   2

3

Modena, gathering together a team of technicians and mechanics to embark on the final phase of his ambition. Racing was the name of the game and any successes would then be interpreted into fast and exotic road going cars.

Over the years he had always admired the twelve cylinder engines which had powered the twin-6 Packards and the V12 Delages, so he was determined that a similar type of unit would be installed in the chassis of his cars. He invited Gioacchino Colombo to design a V12 engine with a single camshaft per bank of cylinders, and a cubic capacity of 1500 cc to comply with the current formula in racing. By 1947 three sports racing cars had been built, designated 125 Competizione, and two were entered for a minor event at Piacenza on 11th May but only one started, driven by Cortese. Ferrari was on his way, and a year later his cars were to compete in Grand Prix races, the first being the Italian Grand Prix over the Valentino Park circuit at Turin on 5th September.

It is now 35 years since cars bearing the Ferrari name first appeared on a race track, and during this time he has taken the Formula 1 Manufacturers' World Championship on nine occasions, his drivers winning a similar number of Drivers' World Championships. On 13 occasions his cars have won Sports Car Championships which, over the years, have been run in various forms. In fact there is not one important race in the calendar that he has failed to win.

There have been the lean years when nothing seemed to go right, but lack of success has always been a great spur to come back and start winning again.

It could be said that he is an enigma with a driving force which few, if any, can fully comprehend and while he will now admit that his emotions towards racing have run somewhat dry, he is still there, a legend in his lifetime, a legend for all time.

THE QUEST FOR SUCCESS

World War Two had barely ended when Ferrari was in business again laying his plans for the Scuderia. Being a man who had built up a vast wealth of knowledge in motor sport as driver, administrator and also in the running of his own organisation, he knew where to find the personnel he needed if the venture was to succeed. He had already decided that the first cars would have a vee twelve configuration, and having worked with Gioacchino Colombo on the successful Alfetta 158 project in 1937 offered him the position of chief designer, with the up and coming young engineer Lampredi as his number two. Among the other personnel was Luigi Bazzi, who had been with Ferrari since the early twenties and was considered the leading development engineer.

The 125F1

Work started on the engine in 1946, and although it was intended that the first cars would be ready for grand prix racing in 1947, it was the sports version which raced first at a minor event at Piacenza in May 1947. The grand prix cars were not seen until 5 September 1948 for the Italian Grand Prix at Valentino Park, Turin, with Giuseppe Farina, Prince 'Bira' and Raymond Sommer as drivers. Sommer brought his car into third place behind Pierre Wimille driving the up-dated Alfa Romeo 158, with Villoresi 2nd in a Maserati. 'Bira' suffered transmission failure and Farina had an argument with some straw bales and retired.

The basic V12 engine was designed to serve three purposes; as a unit for the grand prix and sports racing cars and also to power roadgoing cars. The early Tipo 125 cars as they were designated, failed to fulfil the

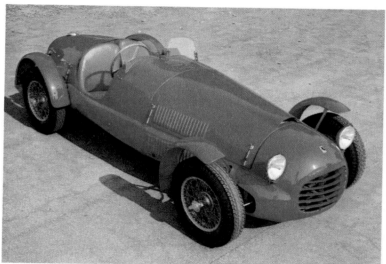

Collins can often be seen in the Cotswold area taking it for an airing, the motor running as sweetly as of old. (3 & 6) One of the earliest known cars to exist, the 166MM Superleggera Touring Spider with chassis No. C0161. Owned by former USA race driver, Briggs Cunningham, the car now resides in his museum in California.

(1, 4 & 5) David Cottingham owns this beautiful 1953 340MM (chassis No. 0350), restored in his own workshop. The two-tone colour of this Vignale bodied spider is the same as when it was delivered to the first owner, Sterling Edwards, an American, who raced this extensively. David Cottingham is not afraid to take to the track with this car, racing it in appropriate events. The 340MM has a 60° V12 sohc engine, with a capacity of 4.1 litres, twin Marelli magnetos and a single plug per cylinder. With three Weber 40 DCF/3 carburettors the power output is 300 bhp at 6600 rpm. (2) An early 166MM with a racing history. The owner Derek

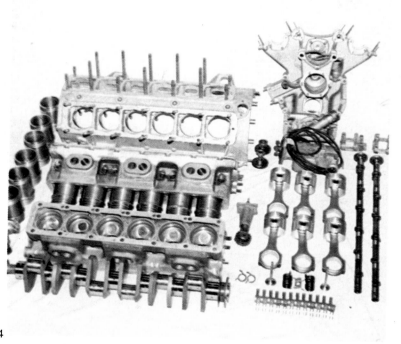

factory's high hopes, but Bazzi was there to sort out the shortcomings. This classic design, in its various derivatives, was to be seen as the power basis for many of the later engines used in a number of the successful road cars, culminating as the unit designed for the 512S and M competition cars of 1970-71.

The original Colombo V12 front-engined formula 1 car had the cylinders at an angle of 60 degrees, and a single overhead camshaft per bank of the cylinders, chain driven from the front, operating a single inlet and single exhaust valve per cylinder, and with a bore/stroke of 55 mm/52.5 mm had a displacement of 1496.7 cc. It was supercharged using a Roots-type blower, which ran at 1.22 times the crankshaft speed. The crankcase and cylinder blocks were aluminium alloy with detachable heads, and the fuel was fed by a single 40 DO3C carburettor located in the 'V' of the engine. Two magnetos, driven from the rear of the camshaft, ignited a single 14 mm plug per cylinder. With a compression ratio of 6.5:1 the power output was 225 bhp at 7000 rpm.

5

6

A five speed and reverse crash gearbox was in unit with a single dry plate clutch, with the drive through an open propshaft to the fixed final drive and exposed half-shafts. The chassis was a tubular frame with oval-section main members, a box section front cross member, and welded tubular upper structure for the bodywork, formed of aluminium panels. Front suspension had a transverse leaf spring with unequal A-arms, while at the rear, single radius arms and torsion bars were used. Houdaille vane-type shock absorbers and hydraulic brakes with finned alloy drums were fitted all round, and the 16 inch centre lock Borrani wire wheels were shod with Pirelli tyres, 5.50-16 at the front and 6.50-16 rear. It had a short wheelbase of 2160 mm with the front track 1255 mm and rear 1200 mm.

Apart from the Italian Grand Prix, during 1948 the car also ran in the Autodrome GP at Monza on 17 October, the Circuit of Garda, Salo, on 24 October and the Penya Rhin GP at Pedralbes, Barcelona, on 31 October. The only success was recorded by Farina, at Salo, winning the race at 72.85 mph (beating a 2-litre Ferrari Spider Corsa driven by Sterzi). Transmission or engine failure caused retirements in the other races, except when Sommer retired at Monza due to illness.

Despite the lack of success, little work was undertaken during the winter months, and it was not until the Italian Grand Prix at Monza on 11 September 1949 that a revised car appeared. There were now twin overhead camshafts per bank of cylinders, twin-stage supercharging, swing axles with exposed half-shafts, and a transverse leaf spring running behind and below the half-shafts, with a single radius arm on each side at the rear. The early car was difficult to handle, so the wheelbase was increased to 2380 mm, the front track to 1270 mm and the rear to 1250 mm, all of which improved the handling characteristics. The new car had a power output of 290 bhp at 7500 rpm.

With the Alfa Romeo team not competing, the Scuderia had a fairly reasonable season, winning the Swiss, Dutch and Czechoslovakian Grand Prix, as well as the Italian GP with the revised car, and running up a number of minor placings. Before the 1949 season started Ferrari had also managed to sign up two of the top drivers, Alberto Ascari and Luigi Villoresi.

While Formula 1 was the premier grade of racing there was also, in the early postwar years, formule libre (for engines of any capacity) and formula 2 (for 2-litre engined cars). The design of the tipo 125 was suitable for conversion to either formula so, for 1949, Ferrari increased the bore and stroke to 60 mm and 58.8 mm for a displacement of 1995 cc. Apart from some minor modifications the formule libre car (designated 166 Formule Libre) had a single Weber 40 DORC carburettor and

A small selection of some of the glamour cars which could only come from the legendary Ferrari stable. (1) The 512M originally owned and raced by Ecurie Francorchamps in 'S' specification. The car has been owned and raced by a number of British drivers and is now fully restored to concours condition by the present owner Nigel Chiltern-Hunt. (2 & 4) The Rocchi designed 4-litre 60 degree V12 330P4 had a number of successes culminating in the Manufacturers' Championship in 1967. The two photographs show the David Clarke car. (3) The David Piper owned 365P2/3.

FORMULA 2 SUCCESS

single-stage supercharger, giving a healthy output of 310 bhp at 7000 rpm while the 166 F2, with the same displacement, had three Weber 32 DCF carburettors but no supercharger and a modest 155 bhp at 7000 rpm. For 1950-51 the F2 power output was raised to 160 bhp. In 1951 the formula 1 car underwent further changes, the bore was increased to 68 mm, the stroke remaining at 58.8 mm, thus raising the cubic capacity to 2562.2 cc. This car was designated 212 F1.

In the early stages of Ferrari development it is by no means easy to follow the variations in the tipos as the whole structure was complex. Engine swapping was common, depending on events entered, so that trying to pinpoint particular chassis to particular races could be a guessing game.

By 1950 the small capacity supercharged engine was having difficulty in keeping ahead of its unblown rivals, since the latter could run a race without refuelling, whereas the thirstier Ferraris lost time by making pit stops to take on fuel. This was not the case as regards the 166 F2 which was unblown and which, during 1950, won 13 of the 15 events entered.

1

2

3

4

(1) Mike Hawthorn in the Dino 246 at the 1958 British GP at Silverstone. He came in 2nd which helped him win the Drivers' World Championship. *(2) The 625F1 car which promised so much but achieved so little. (3 & 5) One of the Harrison brothers' beautifully preserved Ferraris. This is an original 250 Testa Rossa showing its rear view and its pace on the track. (4) An excellent example of the 212 barchetta, a successful sports racing car in the early fifties. There were both road and competition cars, the road cars being referred to as Inter and competition cars as either Export or Sport. (6) The Dino 246F1 which replaced the Ferrari-Lancia cars after their demise in 1957. For some reason the air intakes, which were exposed with a perspex covering, have somehow disappeared under the bonnet!*

However, the Tipo 125 had another poor season in 1950 and in the main it was the British privateer driver, Peter Whitehead, receiving factory support, who upheld the name of Ferrari in formula 1 events.

The 375 F1

During 35 years of designing, building and racing his own cars Ferrari has, at times, shown a reluctance to change the old order, but when he has seen that change would be to his advantage all stops would be pulled out, and such was the flexibility of the factory that a new design could be on the drawing board and in production in record time. It was not suprising therefore, when he dropped the small capacity supercharged formula 1 cars and decided to pin his faith in the unblown 4.5-litre cars, which were eligible under the regulations.

Colombo had meanwhile left Ferrari, returning to Alfa Romeo to see whether he could extract any more power from the now ageing 158/159, and Aurelio Lampredi, who had left earlier, dissatisfied with his original terms of employment, returned with a better deal to replace Colombo. Lampredi was an empirical engineer, a man without professional qualification but with a 'feel' for the subject. He really had a threefold task; to design the 4.5-litre V12 car to beat the Alfa Romeo 159, to design and build an entirely new four cylinder 2.5-litre car for 1954, (when the formula 1 regulations would be changed) and in the interim, a four cylinder 2-litre engine, as Ferrari suspected that for 1952 and 1953 the world championship would revert to formula 2.

As a test bed the 275 F1 3.3-litre 60 degree V12 was developed for the larger capacity unit, and this led to the 4.1-litre 340 F1, followed by the

5

6

THE 375F1

(1) 246F1 at the 1960 Monaco GP
where Phil Hill was placed 3rd. (2) David
Shute's beautifully prepared 225 about to
ascend Prescott Hill. (3) Shark-nosed
156F1 with the 120 degree V6 engine, at
Spa for the 1962 Belgian GP. Phil Hill
was placed 3rd. (4) Another 246F1, in the
pits at the 1960 Monaco GP. (5) The
Ferrari-Lancia 801F1, seen at the 1957
Italian GP at Monza. (6) A medley of
Ferraris lined up for concours judging at

Prescott—far left: a mid-engined 250LM, next: the always well turned-out 166 Spider Corsa of Paul Jackman, an early V12 car with a single overhead camshaft per bank of cylinders and a capacity of 1992 cc. On the right: the 330P4 which was raced by Maranello Concessionaires and subsequently sold to David Clarke. (7) The 1½-litre 120 degree V6 156F1 in the pits prior to the Italian GP at Monza in 1963. Two cars were entered but John Surtees retired with engine failure and Bandini's gearbox packed up. (8) Another early Ferrari, the 166MM, which could be used as either a road car or for competition. The engine was a V12 with a capacity of 1995 cc and the coachwork designed by Giovanni Michelotti for Vignale.

6

7

8

375 F1 with a bore/stroke of 80 mm × 74.5 mm to give a displacement of 4993.7 cc. The chassis and suspension followed the earlier Colombo layout, but at the rear the de Dion tube had become standard. With a single overhead camshaft per bank of cylinders, one inlet and one exhaust valve per cylinder, a single magneto and two plugs per cylinder, three Weber 40 DCF caburettors and a compression ratio of 11:1, the power output in 1950 was 330 bhp at 7000 rpm (raised to 350 bhp for 1951).

During the 1950 season the 375 F1 contested only two events. For the Italian Grand Prix at Monza, on 3 September over 312 miles, two cars were entered, for Ascari and Serafini. The Ascari car had engine failure, but taking over Serafini's car he won the race. At the Penya Rhin GP at Pedralbes on 29 October Ascari won at 93.93 mph, with Serafini second and Pierre Taruffi, driving a 340 F1, third.

1951 saw the return of the Alfa Romeo team, but this would be their final season in grand prix racing for many years and once more it was lack of finance which forced them to quit. The 375 F1 contested 12 important races during the season, winning three of the seven championship grand prix and four of the other races. It was the last race

of the season, the Spanish Grand Prix at Pedralbes, Barcelona, on 28 October which would decide the World Manufacturers and Drivers Championships. Ascari was in pole position with fastest practice time, and Fangio (Alfa Romeo) second fastest. Ferrari should have won, but a tyre choice error caused their downfall and Fangio took the chequered flag with Froilan Gonzales (375 F1) second, and Ascari only fourth. So Alfas and their number one driver, Juan Fangio, had won the season's top awards and Ferrari still had to score his first world championship.

With the withdrawal of the Alfa Romeo team the 375 F1s had no other worthy formula 1 contenders, for the Maseratis, Lago-Talbots and Simcas were outclassed. Most of them were sold off, three to teams which hoped to enter them in the Indianapolis 500 but found, in practice, that the cars hadn't the speed of the specialised Indy cars. A number of these cars exist today in various parts of the world.

The 125S V12, 159 V12, 166 V12 and 500 F2

After World War Two, there were a number of small capacity racing cars which not only had meetings in their own right, but often had a race which would precede the main event (usually for F1 cars) as a

THE FOUR-CYLINDER 500

programme 'filler'. Such cars as the French Simcas and Italian Cisitalias with displacements of 1100 cc provided excellent racing, and the then governing body of motor sport, the Federation Internationale de l'Automobile (F.I.A.), was not slow to recognise that there should be two formulae; one for supercharged 1500 cc and unblown 4.5-litre cars to contest formula 1, the other for unsupercharged cars up to 2-litre (or 500 cc supercharged) for formula 2, both effective from 1 January 1948. Ferrari would, of course, run his 1500 cc supercharged V12 125 F1 in formula 1, but before these cars appeared he had, in 1947, built three 125 Competizione (125C) cars, two with full-width bodies by Touring of Milan and the third with a two-seat body, but with cycle wings. They were designated 125 Sport (125S). The sports racing tipo 159 followed by altering the dimensions of the bore/stroke of the 125C to 59 mm × 58 mm, giving a capacity of 1901 cc. Only two were made, one of which appeared on 15 August 1947 at Pescara driven by Cortese. The 166 series was introduced in 1948 using the tipo 159 engine with the bore enlarged to 60 mm, and with the same stroke the displacement was now 1992 cc, but it was not long before the stroke was altered to 58.8 mm, to give a capacity of 1995 cc. The first cars had cycle type wings and were called Spider Corsa and intended for either sports car racing or formula 2 (the cycle wings and lamps being removed). Later Ferrari had single seat bodied 166 F2 cars built for formula 2 racing.

During 1948, the 1995 cc V12 tipo 166 made six appearances, winning three races and placed second on five occasions. The 1949, 1950 and 1951 were successful seasons for the 166 F2, and this trend was carried into 1952 and 1953 with the entirely new 500 F2.

(1) The Dino 166F2 cars competed in 16 events in 1968 winning 5 races in all. (2) Chris Amon took the 312P to a 4th place in the 1969 Brands Hatch 500, being delayed by tyre and throttle cable problems. (3) The 312F1 of 1968 had a 60 degree V'12 3-litre engine with four valves per cylinder. In its final form the power output was 412 bhp at 10,500 rpm. (4) Minor changes were made to the Dino 166F2 during the 1968 season. Note the absence of wrap-around windscreen and changed exhaust system compared with the car in the top photograph. (5) Jackie Stewart/Chris Amon scored a 2nd place with the 330P4 Spider in the BOAC 500 at Brands Hatch and thereby won the Manufacturers' Championship for Ferrari in 1967. (6) The

For the 1952 and 1953 season the F.I.A. decided that the formula 2 events would count towards the Manufacturers and Drivers World Championships, until the new formula 1 regulations for 2.5-litre cars came into effect in 1954.

Over the years, Ferrari had been more than impressed by the excellent torque characteristics of the four cylinder Alta units which powered the British HWM cars. He instructed Lampredi to produce a four cylinder 2-litre engine for formula 2, and a four cylinder 2.5-litre unit for the forthcoming 1954 formula 1 regulations. This was certainly re-thinking by Ferrari, as the racing world thought he was wedded to a V12 configuration; once more it showed not only his own flexibility, but also that of the design team and factory.

Syracuse GP of 1966 was won by Surtees in a 312F1. The car depicted, a Dino 246 driven by Bandini, was 2nd. (7) Jacky Ickx driving a 312B2 (the B denoting the 180 degree horizontally-opposed 12 cylinder formula 1 cars). It won a share of grand prix but retired too often. Overleaf: Niki Lauda in the 1974 312B3 (chassis No. 010) seen at the Monaco GP, where he retired on lap 32 with ignition trouble.

5

6

7

The new 500 F2 was unveiled by Ferrari in 1951. The 1980 cc four cylinder unit had a bore/stroke of 90 mm × 78 mm, geardriven twin overhead camshafts operating single inlet and exhaust valves per cylinder, two Marelli magnetos to spark the two plugs per cylinder, and four Weber 45 DOE twin-choke carburettors, and with a compression ratio of 12.8 : 1 the power output was 180 bhp at 7500 rpm. The 1951 car had a four-branch exhaust manifold and single pipe, in 1952 four stub exhaust pipes replaced the final single pipe while, for 1953, there were two twin-branch exhaust manifolds leading into a single large diameter pipe.

Two cars were tried out at the Modena Grand Prix on 23 September 1951 which Ascari won at 72.27 mph, while Villoresi retired with engine problems.

There can be little doubt that the 500 F2 was one of Ferrari's more successful designs, as in the two years 1952 and 1953 it won 14 world championships in a row and was only defeated on three occasions in 33

THE LANCIA-FERRARI

races; at Rheims in 1952 by Jean Behra's Gordini, and the Maserati of de Graffenreid and Juan Fangio at Syracuse and Monza respectively in 1953. Alberto Ascari had excelled himself, taking the World Drivers' Championship in two successive years, while Ferrari became World Manufacturers' Champion.

While most Ferraris up to that time were noted for their 'good looks', the 500 F2 was perhaps the most handsome yet seen. It was low built and sleek in the tradition of past racing cars, and it was to be many years before the shape was revolutionised, first by rear-mounted engines and then by the quite ridiculous wide tyres, which give the present day racing cars the appearance of rollerskates.

The Lancia-Ferrari D50

1954 should have been a winning year with the new four cylinder 625 F1, but the Germans had re-entered the grand prix scene with their Mercedes Benz and the Maseratis, while still unreliable, had the speed of the Ferrari. Ferrari had a bad year and while he tried to rebuild his fortunes by introducing the 553 F1 Squalo, which had made its debut in the spring of 1954, and subsequently the 555 F1 Supersqualo and

(1) Clay Regazzoni (left) and Niki Lauda after a pre-race briefing. (2) Lauda during the 1974 Brazilian GP run at Interlagos over 154 miles. The race was cut short due to a violent storm. The 312B3 (chassis No. 012) retired due to misfiring and a broken wing stay. (3) Lauda won the 1975 World Drivers' Championship in the new 312T. (4) Niki Lauda, in the 312B3 (chassis No. 015), led for 73 of the 75 laps in the British GP at Brands Hatch in 1974 when a puncture forced a pit stop. He was not allowed to take his car out again, this depriving him of 5th place. (5) Lauda on his way to 2nd place in the 1974 Brand Hatch Race of Champions. Car 312B3 (chassis No. 012).

interchanged engines, nothing seemed to work. Both the Squalo and Supersqualo were aggressive looking cars, but unfortunately left their aggression on the starting grids.

In the meantime the brilliant automobile engineer and designer Vittorio Jano, who had worked with Enzo Ferrari in the twenties, and finally left the Alfa Romeo concern towards the end of the thirties to join Lancia, had been working on a 2488 cc V8 unit to join the grand prix circus. After much testing, two cars appeared for the final grand prix of 1954, the Spanish, at Pedrales, to be driven by Ascari and Villoresi, both of whom had left Scuderia Ferrari in disgust as they did not fancy driving cars in which they had no hope of winning. At Pedrales Ascari's Lancia showed promise, taking the lead at the start of the race, but on lap 10 his clutch packed up. However, he did have the satisfaction of making fastest lap at 100.80 mph. Villoresi's car did two circuits and then came into the pits with brake failure. The Lancia D50 had a number of novel features including outrigger pontoons, carried on each side of the bodywork between the front and rear wheels, where the main fuel supply was carried, and one of the pontoons carried fuel and also a compartment for oil. Modifications were carried out during

4

5

THE SIX-CYLINDER DINO

the winter of 1954/1955 and although the car contested a number of events in 1955, it never showed its potential.

By the end of May the financial situation at Lancia was desperate and their number one driver, Ascari, was killed while testing a Ferrari sports car at Monza. After much politiking the Italian Automobile Club decreed, on 7 July, that all the D50s and their equipment should be handed over to Scuderia Ferrari, and Vittorio Jano once more found himself employed by Enzo Ferrari. This gesture was a mixed blessing in

The Dino 246 F1

While the 1956 season was in progress Ferrari was looking ahead, as the Ferrari-Lancia was nearing the end of its development and Jano was now supervising the design and production of an all-new 65 degree V6 1500 cc engine to contest the 1958 formula 2 races. Appearing at Posillipo for the Naples Grand Prix on 28 April 1957 and running out of its class, as the race was for formula 1 cars, it put up a spirited performance, finishing third behind Peter Collins and Mike Hawthorn

many ways, for Ferrari had been racing the 625s, 553s and 555s in a variety of combinations and while the Lancia D50 had yet to prove itself, he did at least have some 'material' on which to work and also Jano who had conceived the car. A great deal of work on the cars took place during the close season of 1955-56, including the enlargement of the bore to 76 mm and reduction of the stroke to 68.5 mm, all of which paid off for the new season. Additionally, the 'new' Ferrari-Lancia 801 with an increased output of 275 bhp at 8200 rpm was ready by the spring. In all, 1956 was a good season, for the works not only had Juan Fangio as the number one driver but they also won five of the seven races counting towards the championship, and Fangio became World Driver Champion. In spite of this, Fangio left the scuderia at the end of the season as he was convinced that the cars he was given to drive were inferior to those allotted to other team members.

Although the Ferrari-Lancias, in a variety of forms, contested 11 races in 1957, they were successful in only one major grand prix, the other successes were at Syracuse and Naples. There were many retirements through engine and clutch failures and three cars were involved in crashes at the Monaco Grand Prix. All told, a somewhat depressing season.

driving Ferrari-Lancia 801s. In July, at Rheims, Maurice Trintignant took the car to victory over the 'new breed' of rear-engined Coopers in the Coupe de Vitesse.

Such performances convinced Ferrari that he was on the right lines if the car was to be developed for formula 1 racing, and before the season ended, two of the engines were bored out to 1860 cc to produce 215 bhp. At Modena in October, in spite of giving away 600 cc to the Maseratis, the cars finished second and fourth. To end the season, the Moroccan Grand Prix (last held in 1930) for formula 1 cars was run at Casablanca, and the works entered two Dinos with enlarged engines. Hawthorn's car had a displacement of 2195 cc while Collins had a full-blown formula 1 engine, with a capacity of 2417 cc and said to develop 290 bhp at 8300 rpm. Collins led from lap 1 until he spun on lap 8; unfortunately he spun for a second time at the same corner on lap 16 and retired with damaged bodywork. Hawthorn was struggling in eighth place and by lap 10 he was in the pits with an apparently broken piston, and it was also noticed that the gearbox casing was split.

In 1958 the 246 F1 was prefixed with Ferrari's late son's name Dino, and all V6 engines thereafter were so named. Between 1957 and 1960 there were nine variations of the Dino 246 F1, including the Dino 256 F1,

2

3

4 September 1960. Admittedly the British contingent had stayed at home, objecting to the use of the banked area which they considered too rough for their cars' suspensions, however, it is doubtful whether any other team could have defeated them on the day.

The 156 F1

Ferrari did not send any cars across the Atlantic for the United States Grand Prix at Riverside Raceway, California, as he had too much work on hand preparing for the 1961 season. Having been finally convinced that the future lay in rear-engined cars, he had had his first prototype at Monaco in 1960, using the 2.4-litre V6 unit and other parts from the Dino 246 F1. Richie Ginther drove, but the car was not competitive and retired with final drive failure. By July 1960 Ferrari had a 1.5-litre V6 car ready, the Dino 156 F2, and sending it to the Solitude Ring, West Germany, for a 142 mile race, von Trips not only won the race against

*(1, 2 &3) **Three fine shots of the diminutive Gilles Villeneuve in the turbo-charged 126C V6 1½-litre car (chassis No. 052). From the 'graffiti' carried on the car should be noted the growing influence of FIAT. The early turbo cars had been prone to suffer from 'lag', a lack of response to the throttle when accelerating, but by the time of the 1981 Monaco GP (when these pictures were taken) this 'turbo lag' had almost been cured.**
**For many laps the 126C struggled as the handling, never satisfactory, grew worse as the 'skirts' disintegrated. The leading cars also had problems and when Alan Jones (Williams) had to refuel Villeneuve took him on lap 72 and retained his lead for the remaining four laps. Overleaf: A fine head-on view of Villeneuve with the 126C.*

but in a number of instances the modifications carried out during the four years were not drastic.

1958 was not only an exciting and reasonably successful year, it was also a tragic year for Ferrari. Although Mike Hawthorn only won the French Grand Prix at Rheims, he scored sufficient points in the other events to win the World Drivers' Championship. After becoming champion he retired, but time was running out for him and he met his death on the Guildford by-pass, while driving his 3.4-litre Jaguar, on 22 January 1959. Musso met his death at Rheims; while taking a right-hander at too great a speed, the car hit the grass verge and he was thrown out when it rolled. At the Nurburgring for the German Grand Prix, Peter Collins was killed when travelling a shade too fast at the right-hand bend in the Pflanzgarten and, hitting the bank, rolled his car over the hedge.

While the Dino 246 F1 had its 'moments' during the next two seasons, it went into a gradual decline as the lightweight rear-engined British contenders took command of the circuits. But it went out in a blaze of glory with the American drivers Phil Hill and Richie Ginther and the Belgian Willy Mairesse taking the first three places in the Italian Grand Prix, run over the road and banked section at Monza on

strong opposition, but also broke the lap record. For 1961 there were two versions of the 156 F1 car; the 65 degree and 120 degree V6. The former had a bore/stroke of 73 mm × 59.1 mm giving a displacement of 1481.1 cc, and the latter had a shorter stroke of 58.8 mm and the displacement 1476.6 cc. With two Weber 40 1F3C carburettors, chain driven twin-overhead camshaft, twin coils and a distributor, 2 plugs per cylinder and a compression ratio of 9.8 : 1 it had an output of 190 bhp at 9500 rpm. On the whole 1961 could be considered as a good year since Phil Hill, by winning the Belgian and Italian Grand Prix events, and scoring enough points in other championship races, became the first American to win a Drivers' World Championship. It was also a good year for the young Italian Giancarlo Baghetti, who rose to stardom for one season by winning at Syracuse and Naples and to everyone's surprise beat the field for the important French Grand Prix at Rheims on 2 July, over a distance of 268 miles. Baghetti was using the 65 degree V6 engine.

Tragedy, however, struck again during the year for, on the second lap of the Italian Grand Prix, Jim Clark and von Trips, approaching the Parabolica curve, collided. Clark's Lotus spun out of harm's way onto the grass verge but von Trips' Ferrari catapulted up the grass bank throwing him out and he died without regaining consciousness. The car

(1) *Villeneuve's new 126C2 (chassis No. 055) at the 1982 South African GP. Harvey Postlethwaite had designed a new chassis and while the two KKK turbochargers were retained, other changes included a revised suspension system and narrower gearbox. The Goodyear Tyre Co. had re-entered the grand prix scene so Ferrari switched from Michelins feeling he would get a better deal from them. (2, 3, 4*

which would form part of the chassis, thus adding strength to the structure. As the V8 was not ready for testing, a V6 engine was installed and fitted with Bosch high-pressure fuel injection, with the pump located in the vee. The new chassis followed Lotus practice, and was formed by two pontoons which held the fuel and ran from the front suspension to the rear of the driving compartment. To give added strength there were four tubes in each pontoon. The new chassis, with a redesigned 120 degree V6 engine, appeared at Monza in practice for the Italian Grand Prix, to be run on the road circuit on 8 September. Driven

& 5) It is now many years since the factory has been directly involved in the great annual 24-hour Le Mans race as no suitable cars were available and the cost of developing a car would be astronomical. However, year after year, Ferrari has been represented by their concessionaires as well as privateers, most of whom have been given some support from Modena. Both Ch. Pozzi of Paris and the North American Racing Team have entered the roadgoing 512BBs suitably modified for the endurance test. Success has not always come their way but in the main the 512BB has put up reasonable performances. Three cars which competed in 1981 are shown. Car No. 46 was shared by P. Dieudonne/ J. Xhenceval/J-P. Libert; car No. 45 by F. Violati/M. Flammini/D. Truffo and the Ch. Pozzi car No. 47 by J-C. Andruet/ C. Ballot-Lena/H. Regout.

was hurled against the wire-mesh fence behind which many spectators were watching; eleven were killed and a number of others injured.

After this debut by the 156 F1, which had an unusual nose (two large air intake nostrils giving it a shark-like appearance), disaster struck. There was an unholy row at Marenello, with the chief engineer, Carlo Chiti, team manager, Tavoni, and other senior staff staging a walkout. No reason for the row has ever leaked out, but development work during the winter of 1961 was minimal and this was reflected in the 1962 results without a single major victory.

During the summer of 1963 Ferrari was testing a new monocoque chassis for the proposed rear-mounted 90 degree V8 unit of 1487.5 cc

by John Surtees (a seven times winner of the World Motorcycle Championship), it achieved fastest lap and took the pole position. However, his race was run by lap 17, when a piston failed after contact with a broken valve.

The 158 F1

By April 1964 the first 158 F1 was hastily assembled and without any testing rushed off to Siracusa for the Syracuse Grand Prix held on 12 April. Surtees brought the car into first place averaging 102.63 mph while Bandini, using a V6 car, followed him home. Success with the new car was slow in coming, having suffered a number of retirements, but on 2 August at the Nurburgring for the German Grand Prix, the V8 'came on song'. Surtees won at 96.57 mph and although the car failed at Saltweg for the Austrian event, it won again at the all-important Italian Grand Prix at Monza on 6 September, averaging 127.77 mph. For the United States and Mexican Grand Prix Surtees could only place the 158 F1 in second spot. For a new design, the season could be considered reasonably successful, and Surtees had amassed sufficient points to win the World Drivers' title and the factory, the Manufacturers' title.

Before the season ended, the new flat-12 or boxer type engine was given an airing during practice for the Italian race. Bandini drove, but the car was 'put away' and did not line up on the grid. Designated tipo 1512 it had a capacity of 1489 cc and a claimed power output of 225 bhp. During 1965 the flat 12 engined car shared the grid with the 158 F1 in all the races contested, but neither car won a race throughout the season.

The 312 V12

For 1966, the F.I.A. changed the formula 1 regulations to embrace engines with a limit of 3000 cc unblown, or 1500 cc supercharged. Ing. Rocchi was given the job of designing the engine for the new car, and with so much experience of V12 units (the majority of the sports racing and roadgoing cars had stuck with the V12), he decided on this configuration for the tipo 312 cars. Unfortunately, the cars, whilst not total failures, had little success and between 1966 and 1969 won only two major grand prix, so it was no wonder that New Zealander Chris Amon, decided to quit the team.

In fact the lean years persisted, and it was not until 1975 that both the Manufacturers' and Drivers' titles came Ferrari's way once more. Eleven years was a long time, but it all adds up to the fact that Enzo Ferrari was never a man to call it a day, however much the odds were stacked against him.

The 312B and 312T series

A new wave of cars was to come from the factory in 1970, and although it was some years before they became really competitive, the 312B (B for

1

2

3

4

A mixture of elegant 1960s road cars and the more brutal but handsome sports racing cars of the fifties. (1 & 7) The not too successful 6-cylinder in line 121LMs. (2) The beautiful V12 275GTB/2 was in production between 1964 and 1966 when some 460 were produced. (4 & 6) Photographs show the spider model of the 275. (3 & 5) The 750 Monza 4-cylinder 3-litre engine was derived from the 555 engine and the sleek bodywork was from a design by Ferrari's son Dino. The car was not an overall racing success, being somewhat unpredictable to drive.

'boxer' the German term for a horizontally-opposed engine) was being tested prior to the 1969 Italian Grand Prix, in the hope that it would run in the event. However, it did not appear until 7 March 1970 for the South African (non-championship) Grand Prix at Kyalami, when Jacky Ickx retired due to falling oil pressure. The 312 B owed its ancestry to the flat-12 tipo 1512 which was seen in action during 1965, and also the tipo 212E (flat-12) used by Peter Schetty, who took this car to victory in the 1969 European Hill Climb Championship. The boxer engine was not only lighter in weight than the V12, but a great deal more compact. With a bore/stroke of 78.5 mm × 51.5 mm the displacement was 2991 cc. The twin overhead camshafts per bank of cylinders were driven by gear,

and operated two intake and two exhaust valves per cylinder. Ignition was by Marelli transistor and fuel injection by Lucas, and, with a compression ratio of 11.8 : 1, a healthy output of 455 bhp was available at 11,500 rpm. The 312 B with minor design changes was in series up to B3 unit (1974-1975). Its greatest successes were achieved in 1970, when Jacky Ickx won three (the Austrian, Canadian and Mexican) and Clay Regazzoni won one (the Italian) of the last five grand prix of the season. But such successes were not to be repeated.

Generally speaking the lack of success of these cars could be put down, to some extent, to the fact that Ferrari was, for part of the time, engaged in the Sports racing car championship, and therefore there was

5

6

7

a division of his recources. On the other hand, the 312PB cars used the flat-12 engine, but detuned so as to last the somewhat longer distances these cars raced.

By late 1974 the new T boxer was shown to the press, (T standing for Transversale, meaning transverse gearbox) and Ferrari now had a car capable of winning. With Niki Lauda and Clay Regazzoni as his drivers, he was once more in the ascendant. 1975 was a good year, with Lauda winning the World Drivers' Championship and the factory taking the Manufacturers' title. During the year, the authorities decreed that the high air intake behind the driver would be banned during 1976, so the car had to be revamped for the Spanish Grand Prix. The new car was designated the 312T2. Lauda continued his run of successes during

1

3

4

(1) The interior seating arrangement of the luxurious 365GTB/4, more commonly known as the Daytona. It had a long production line of some 1300 models turned out between 1968 and 1973 and is certainly one of the legendary Ferraris. There was also a spider version which is much sought after. (2, 3 & 4) Probably one of the most popular production models ever to come from the factory, the 308GTB (also in spider form) is a 3-litre 4 cam V8 with the engine laid transversely at the rear. The elegant flowing lines are derived from the original 206GT through the 246GT/GTS series. A design which can hardly be faulted, the model superseded the 246GT series in 1975 and with slight modifications is still in production, although the carburettors have now been abandoned in favour of a fuel injection system. For the first two years the coachwork was of fibreglass.

5

6

8

7

(5, 6, 7, 8 & 9) Unlike the majority of Ferraris, which have been designed by Pininfarina, the 250GT Spider California came from the drawing-boards of Scaglietti, who have been responsible for building most of the bodies since the late 1950s. The California is a most desirable car, with lines that are difficult to fault. In all about 125 models were produced between 1958 and 1963, in both short and long wheelbase versions, and the car was powered by a 3-litre V12 engine producing 250 bhp at 7000 rpm.

1976, but after winning in Brazil, South Africa, Belgium and Monaco, tragedy overtook him in the German Grand Prix at the Nurburgring, when he was seriously injured in a ghastly accident. His indomitable spirit pulled him through, and to everyone's amazement he was back racing before the end of the season, competing in the last three grand prix. With the points gained, Ferrari took the Manufacturers' championship.

Lauda was still in winning form with the 312T2 in 1977, and in taking the South African, German and Dutch events and being placed in a number of other races, he won his second World Drivers' Championship and once more Ferrari gained another Manufacturers' title. Nonetheless, the season ended on a sour note as the relationship between Lauda and Enzo Ferrari, always delicately balanced, finally broke down at the United States Grand Prix at Watkins Glen, when Lauda walked away from motor racing.

Carlos Reutemann became number one driver for the Scuderia in 1978, with the young French Canadian Gilles Villeneuve as his team mate, but neither could emulate the successes of the previous three seasons. It was left to Jody Scheckter and Villeneuve to retrieve the

9

(1 & 3) *The ex Peter Collins 250GT* Spider now completely restored after languishing under a tree, the resin from which ruined the coachwork. The car has been rebuilt with a special transmission suitable for hill climb competition. (2) Interior of John Fazackerley's concours 250GT cabriolet.

(4 & 5) Hans Asberg's immaculate 365BB seen at the Honington Hall concours 1981. Two days previously the car had been raced at the Ferrari Owners' Club Test Day at the Donington circuit. The 365 berlinetta boxer (flat 12 engine) has a capacity of 4.4 litres and produces 380 bhp at 7,500 rpm. In production from 1973, it was superseded by the more powerful 5-litre 512BB. A handsome car much sought after by enthusiasts. (6 & 7) There was a very limited production run of these sleek, handsome cars, with only 37 built between 1964 and 1966. The 500 Superfast was not only designed but also built by Pininfarina. The 5-litre V12 engine only had a single camshaft per bank of cylinders but could put out a hefty 500 bhp at 6500 rpm. A few of the later cars had optional air-conditioning and power steering. The car shown was owned by Ken Bradshaw.

situation in 1979, with the T3 and T4 cars. Scheckter won the Belgian, the Monaco and Italian races thus securing the World Drivers' awards, with Villeneuve runner-up and the factory winning the Manufacturers' Championship.

Scheckter and Villeneuve teamed up again for 1980, but nothing seemed to go right and Scheckter, seeming to have lost some of his fire, retired at the end of the season.

The 126C and 126C2

During the early part of the year, rumour was rife that Ferrari would have a 1500 cc V6 turbo car ready before the end of the season. The press had a preview on 9 June of an experimental car. The V was at 120 degrees, with the turbochargers and exhausts within the V, which would create a big build-up of heat and therefore dispersion problems. These were admitted by the designer, Mauro Forghieri, and to overcome them there were lateral louvres in the high engine cover and two extra radiators mounted in the side pods. Ferrari admitted to getting 540 bhp from the unit, and at 7500 rpm, 100 bhp more than the flat-12 version car. The 1496.4 cc engine has a bore/ stroke of 81 mm × 48.4 mm, fuel system is Lucas injection and at the end of the 1981 season there were still two KKK turbo chargers, but other methods of turbocharging are at the experimental stage. While Renault, with their 90 degree V6 turbocharged engine, seem to have found more reliability,

there is still some way to go to extract maximum power and reliability. The present disadvantages of the turbo are: (1) slow engine response in acceleration, which now seems to have been solved; (2) low power output at low revs, which is directly related to the turbocharger's rotations; (3) lack of turbocharger reliability since it turns at around 135,000 rpm; (4) difficulty in finding the correct air/fuel mixture for all conditions and also cooling; (5) heat build-up and mechanical loads, using current metals.

With Scheckter retired, Ferrari offered the vacant team place to Didier Pironi for the 1981 season, alongside Villeneuve. Apart from Villeneuve making pole position for the San Marino Grand Prix, however, there were no successes until the Monaco race, when he won at 82.039 mph. To everyone's surprise Villeneuve triumphed again, at the Spanish event held on the twisty Jarama circuit on 21 June. But there were to be no further wins for the rest of the season and although the handling of the cars was atrocious, it was not the only reason for their failure. Something had to be done about the poor handling, so, during the winter of 1981 Ferrari called in Harvey Postlethwaite, a chassis and suspension expert from Britain. A new chassis has been designed using carbon fibre for the front and rear bulkheads, and aluminium honeycomb for the monocoque, with the materials glued together. Weight has been reduced to under 590 kilos, (a saving of some 50 kilos over the 1981 car) and more power extracted from the engine, a claimed

(1, 3 & 4) The 246GT in the early *production days was not exactly a well put together car but by dint of hard work most of the models around today are of concours standard, having been restored to perfection by their current owners. The V6 2.4-litre engine was produced in the* *FIAT factory and it also powered the almost invincible Lancia Stratos Rally cars. (2 & 5) The lovely 206SP which is also depicted on pages 12 and 13.*

580 bhp. Front and rear suspensions have been revised and a narrower transverse gearbox fitted. The new car still uses two KKK turbochargers and is now designated 126C2. It is amusing to reflect that as there is no 'th' in Italian, the personnel at Modena find the name Postlethwaite a tongue twister and settle for 'Ah, Dottore Harvey'. Enzo Ferrari, however, finds no difficulty and it is to Postlethwaite's credit that he is rapidly learning to speak Modenese Italian.

Ferrari has never concerned himself solely with single seat racing, and the list of triumphs for the World Sports Car Championship outstrip the formula 1 constructors titles he has won. The following tells the story:—

1953 (340MM and 375MM), 1954 (375MM, 500 Mondial, 375 Plus and 750 Monza), 1956 (860 Monza and 290MM), 1957 (290MM, 335 Sport and 315S), 1958 (250 Testa Rossa), 1960 (250 Testa Rossa and Dino 246), 1961 (250 Testa Rossa and Dino 246SP).

With a change of emphasis in the championship, he won the 1962 and 1963 titles with gran turismo cars and during the period commencing 1962, prototype cars were included, which extended his championship wins to 1965, 1967 and finally 1972.

THE MODULO

From the time Enzo Ferrari set up his Scuderia in December 1929, he became totally involved with motor racing, initially by racing the cars provided by his former employers, Alfa Romeo, and after the 1940-1945 war by designing and building cars bearing his own name.

Devotion to an ideal of this kind necessitates a deep purse, for while the rewards can be great, the expense can be even greater and it is not every year that a constructor can produce a winning formula, for, in reality, there are more 'downs' than 'ups'. In 1947, when Ferrari started racing his own cars, there were no great financial prizes to be won, nor were there large sums of money available from sponsorship, but he managed to keep going with quite a few successes, plus the sale of surplus racing and sports racing cars. In late 1950 Ferrari introduced the first of his road going cars, the 2.5 litre 212 Inter, of which some 35 to 37 were built. This was followed in 1953 with the first of the 250 series, the 3 litre Europa, which was produced in a variety of tipos, so that by the end of their run, some 11 years later, the total production of all cars from the factory had reached a figure of over 3000. It was the 250 series on which Ferrari really built his name, and, without doubt, became the greatest constructor of racing, GT and sports racing cars the world has ever known. So, without the support of cars for sale in those days, it is doubtful whether even Ferrari could have financed his extensive racing programme year after year.

From 1947 until 1972 Ferrari was to pursue a two-headed racing programme which, at times, resulted in his resources being over-stretched. The premier prize was, of course, always the Formula I Manufacturers' World Championship instituted in 1950 and which he has won on nine occasions. The other major prize, certainly up to 1972, was the World Sports Car Championship started in 1953 and continued until 1961 when it was replaced by a series of championships concerned, at first, with GT cars, but which developed into races for prototypes of either GT or sports cars. During 19 years of the championship contested by Ferrari, he claimed the title no fewer than 16 times.

(1, 2 & 3) Called the Modulo, this is without doubt one of the wildest designs ever executed on a chassis which was developed for a sports racing GT car. The total simplicity of the interior and exterior could only have been conceived by the team of artistic and architecturally motivated men from Pininfarina.

In fact, Ferrari's record in what could be termed the classic sports car races from 1948, has been most impressive and it is true to say that his cars have won every major track event in the motor racing calendar, a number of them on many occasions.

While the fifties were a fruitful time, it is worth noting that one of the greatest periods of GT and also prototype racing developed in the sixties, when, it cannot be denied, Ferrari produced a series of cars which were probably the most exciting the world has ever seen on the racing circuits.

The GT cars raced in this period were the successors to the 250 series, starting with the short wheel base 250 GT berlinetta derived from the long wheel base 250 GT, which dominated the classes in 1956, 1957

4

5

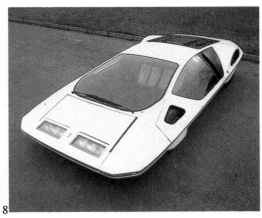

6

7

8

(4 to 8) Pininfarina have for years been noted for their artistry in designing coachwork for cars and perhaps their most notable styling creations have been executed on Ferraris. This is not surprising when so many of the cars have been classics in engineering, and a legend has been built up around the cars and their

creator Enzo Ferrari. The Modulo was designed around the 512S chassis and although impractical as shown, with slight modifications to the wheel arches and rear vision, it could in all probability have taken not only to the track but also the road.

the legendary Enzo Ferrari was at the heart of it.

Before the end of the era, at the November 1969 Turin show, Pininfarina showed, in his inimitable style, the next generation of Ferraris to take to the circuits. There was a berlinetta *speciale* on a 512 chassis; impracticable as either a road or racing car, it was an exercise in craftsmanship and one of the wildest designs ever thought up by a coachbuilder. The line from bonnet front to the top of the windscreen was no more than 12 degrees from the horizontal and the roof line, extending over the mid-engine compartment, was a hardly perceptible parabolic curve ending in a sharp cut-off tail. More was to follow, for in March 1970 Pininfarina, still using the 512 chassis, had dreamt up a more wayout design which he called the Modulo.

This exercise could be described as being conceived by both an artist and architect, without any thought for its practical use. In fact, it would not have been possible to see out of the rear screen and it could only have travelled in a straight line or, at best, it might have negotiated a protracted, gentle curve. The front wheels were enclosed within the outside body panels and the inner panels would have permitted only minimal lateral movement. The overall line can be described as flowing, from the bonnet to the Kamm type rear end, and the maximum height

and 1958. This tipo was followed up by the 250 GTO in two series and the 330 LMB, both of which were front engined V12s. These cars were replaced by a bewildering array of mid-engined V12 prototypes, the 250 P, 250 LM, 275 P, 330 P, 275 P2, 330 P2, 365 P2 and P2/3, 330 P3, 330 P4, 412 P (330 P 3/4) and 250 P5, some of which were for racing by customers and some as show pieces. Perhaps the success that Ferrari achieved was due to the fact that he seldom built an all new car. The engine might be new, or even located in a different position or a new gearbox installed, or again an all new suspension. It would seem that whatever combination was used for the prototypes, success was generally to be found around the corner. This superb era in motor racing had to come to an end, but it is one not likely to be forgotten, and was no more than 3' 8". The windscreen, together with the roof section and side windows, formed a complete unit, and the whole glided forward to allow driver and passenger entry and exit. Unlike the current fashion on a number of exotic cars, the front lamps were not of the 'pop-up' type, since this would have interfered with the overall flowing line, so they were recessed behind perspex covers. The rear set of lights were encased in horizontal slots on either side of the tail, and being recessed kept even the rear end smooth and free from any protrusion.

While these two cars were being designed and used at shows to promote Pininfarina, Ferrari's intent was of course more serious and the first 512 S competition car was put on view at his annual press conference at Maranello in December 1969, having started on the project the previous April with FIAT money. He planned to field three car for the major events in 1970 with the intention of regaining the Manufacturers' World Championship.

Now the heart of any Ferrari has always been its power plant, and the engine of the 512 S (S for Sport) was based on the castings of the

The races, instituted in 1966, were contested by both American and European sports cars driven by professionals and amateurs, and were essentially an end of season series starting in September and going through to November. The 7 litre Group 7 Chevrolet engine was the most favoured power plant, with plenty of torque throughout its range, so participation by the Ferraris, which were well down on torque, was something of a gamble.

However, in 1967 Luigi Chinetti, the Ferrari Concessionaire in America and head of the North American Racing Team, decided to enter his 330 P3/4 in the series and returned the car to the works at Modena, Italy to be prepared for the races. It is doubtful whether any mechanical modifications were carried out but the overall weight was trimmed and the body lowered.

Ludovico Scarfiotti had the drive in its first race at Bridgehampton on 17th September and was not disgraced with a 7th place against some tough opposition from the McLarens and Lolas using Chevrolet engines. At Mosport, Scarfiotti was delayed on the grid with problems which later led to his retirement.

Ferrari Can Am cars and particularly the 612 Can Am, the cubic capacity of which was finally increased to a near 7 litres, so with a new engine limit of 5 litres for the sports car championship which had come into effect on 1st January 1968, the unit was to prove durable. A further regulation stipulated that 50 cars had to be built for homologation, but both Ferrari and Porsche, the main contenders, protested so the figure was reduced to 25.

Since the 512 S was based on the Ferrari Can Am cars, a brief reference to the races of this series held on the circuits of North America and Canada and relating to Ferrari participation would be appropriate.

In the factory at Modena. (1) The assembly line with 512BBi cars awaiting wheels and other pieces of equipment before proceeding to the shop floor where (2) a female worker takes over and spends all her time cleaning and polishing the cars before they are ready for distribution to the worldwide network of concessionaires. (3) A further assembly line, this time of 308GTB/GTS fuel injection cars. (4) Work goes ahead on assembling the power plants with a 4.8-litre V12 400GTi in the foreground. In the background, work proceeds on the flat 12 512BBi engine.

Back at Modena, Ferrari prepared two new Group 7 prototypes; these were 330 P4s which were lightened and the overall engine capacity increased to 4176 cc (bore 79 mm and stroke 71 mm) with the output 480 bhp at 8500 rpm. The cars were entered by the American West Coast

4

distributor, Bill Harrah, and designated type 350 Can Am/350 P4. The factory gave their full support. Chris Amon and Jonathan Williams were the drivers and at Laguna Seca Amon came in 5th and Williams 8th, both respectable placings considering the displacement and power the cars were giving away to their competitors. At the Riverside race Amon finished 9th, while Williams spun and in the process was shunted by Peter Revson's Lola-Chevrolet. Their last race was at Las Vegas for the Stardust Grand Prix, which resulted in both cars being non-finishers. Williams' car was out early, having ingested dust and stones in the air intake when Muther's Lola spun in front of him at the first turn.

Amon, however, was on the last lap when he and Morley, in a Lola, had a shunt resulting in the Ferrari colliding with a bridge strut, thus putting him out of the race.

Ferrari's competition engineer, Mauro Forghieri, was obviously impressed with the performance of his underpowered cars and decided that a 6 litre engine would give the Scuderia a better chance of winning some of the races the following season. The new 612 Ferrari was awaited eagerly as each race in the 1968 series approached, but it was not until the final round at Las Vegas that it appeared. The displacement was now 6222 cc (bore 92 mm and stroke 78 mm) and with Lucas indirect fuel injection together with a 10.5 : 1 compression ratio and 48 valves the V12 unit produced 620 bhp at 7000 rpm. Amon was at the wheel but his race was run at the first turn, when the leading cars piled into each other and once more dirt was sucked into the air intake necessitating retirement. A revamped 612 was ready for the 1969 season and at Watkins Glen Amon posted a 3rd place behind the McLarens of Denis Hulme and Bruce McLaren, and at the Edmonton event he finished 2nd, a mere 5 seconds behind Hulme. Still competitive, he was third at the Mid-Ohio race with the almost untouchable McLarens up front, but on this occasion he was running with the underpowered 1968 engine. A piston had collapsed in the new unit during practice, and with half-hearted factory support and lacking spares, the engine had to be returned to Italy for repair. At Elkhart Lake, still using the old engine, Amon retired six laps from the finish when the fuel pump gave up. Bridgehampton followed but the old engine was now tired, and although Amon was third fastest in practice he retired on lap three.

By the time the Michigan race came round the repaired 6.2 litre engine had been returned from Italy, but during a late practice session a rod-bearing failed so Amon had to sit-out the race. Repairs were effected for Laguna Seca and on this occasion the oil pump failed, again during practice, and the car non started. An all-new 6.9 litre engine was sent over from the factory and installed in time for the Riverside event, so the car was now designated type 712. Despite oil cooling problems during practice, Amon made third fastest time. However, with the car on the grid the starter button failed, so Amon had an illegal push start and was black flagged, which meant the end of his race. The only other event the 712 contested was at the Texas International Speedway, where 3

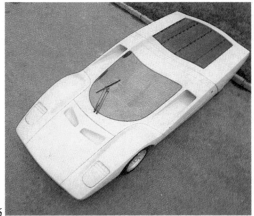

(4, 5, 6 & 7) The 512S Speciale was another Pininfarina styling exercise based on Ferrari's 512 chassis which was to contest the Manufacturers' Championship in 1970 and 1971. This design appeared at the Turin Show in November 1969. It had long rising fenders from aft the front wheel arches, and the windshield, with a slope of 78 degrees and containing the engine air intakes at the rear, was built to lift forward in one piece allowing driver entry and exit. Overleaf: The berlinetta boxer 512 is considered the world's supercar and flagship of the Ferrari range. The flat 12 engine produces 360 bhp at 6,800 rpm.

(1, 2 & 3) Three views of the 512M (chassis No. 1030) raced by Ecurie Francorchamps during 1970 and 1971 in S specification. After finishing 8th at the Spa 1000 km event it was returned to the factory and fitted with a 'Coda Lunga' (long tail) body for Le Mans, where it finished 5th. At the season's end it contested the Kyalami 9-hours race, finishing 6th. During 1971 it was entered in the following races: Buenos Aires (1000 km), Daytona 24-hour, Le Mans and the Watkins Glen 6-hour and Can Am.

it lost a piston in practice and non started, so Amon reverted to the 612 but retired after 10 laps. So ended Ferrari's involvement in the Can Am series.

Although Mauro Forghieri had seemed enthusiastic over the Can Am series at the close of the 1968 season, there was little doubt that Enzo Ferrari had already lost interest. In fact it is doubtful whether his heart was ever in the project, as he was known not to favour racing in the Americas, even if he had to make occasional forays by supporting such races as the 24 hour Daytona and 12 hour Sebring events. In general terms it could be said that he was quite happy to allow his dealers or concessionaires, such as Luigi Chinetti with his North American Racing Team, to represent the Marque in the States. It is true he did provide a 6.2 litre car for 1969 and also an up-dated 6.9 litre engine, but he had virtually abandoned his works driver, Chris Amon, who was left to find his own mechanics and other personnel to keep the team running.

There is no reason to speculate on his lack of interest for it is obvious that he had obtained sufficient information for the Scuderia's next objective, the winning of the 5-litre Group 5 Sports Car Championship in 1970 with the 512 S.

The power plant of the 512 S was a typical and classic Ferrari design, and as matters stand at present, was no doubt to be the final competition vee twelve. The 60 degree double overhead camshaft V12 engine had a bore of 87 mm and stroke of 70 mm giving an overall displacement of 4994 cc; indirect fuel injection by Lucas, 48 valves and a single 10 mm sparking plug for each cylinder. A single Marelli distributor, driven by the left intake camshaft at the rear of the engine, provided the ignition and with an 11.8 : 1 compression ratio the output was 500 bhp at 8500 rpm. Four fuel pumps fed the injection system and these were driven by the right intake camshaft. Water radiators were located on either side of the engine with the oil coolers in the nose.

The crankcase and most other parts of the engine were from light alloy castings. Each bank of cylinders had a water pump driven from the main gear train and there was one pressure and two scavenger oil pumps. The engine was mounted at the rear but ahead of the rear axle, in unit

with the 5-speed all synchromesh and reverse gearbox with limited slip differential. The clutch was multi-disc and brakes Girling disc, but without servo assistance.

The tubular steel with aluminium skin chassis frame had a wheelbase of 2400 mm, front track of 1518 mm and rear track 1511 mm. Campagnolo centre-lock alloy wheels were used, shod with Firestone 4.75/11.50 X 15 tyres at the front and 6.00/14.50 X 15 at the rear.

Suspension was all independent with unequal length A arms in front, while at the rear the lower arm was reversed to locate the wheel alignment. Coil springs and Koni shock absorbers were fitted all round and steering was by rack and pinion.

different body styles. The Press conference car had a louvred white panel covering the engine compartment and the slightly upswept tail had a barely perceptible spoiler, and apart from the normally placed headlamps in the wings, it had two additional driving lights placed low and in the centre of the nose. For the Daytona race the tail had been completely modified with fins and a large spoiler, and to increase front end stability the cars which appeared at Sebring had their noses lowered to give a more squared off look when seen from the side. At the same time scoops had been cut to feed cool air to the fuel pumps, as fuel delivery problems had beset the cars at Daytona. The fuel injection system had been modified to produce an extra 40 bhp and chassis

(1) In the foundry. Casting the heads for the flat 12 engines. (2) A stack of cylinder-heads, destined for the 4 camshaft V8 engine, ready for final touches before assembly. These engines have the V at 90 degrees and a bore/stroke of 81mm/71mm giving a capacity of 2926cc, are used for both the 308GTBi/GTSi and the Mondial 8. Bosch K-jetronic fuel injection is standard but the 308 series put out some 255 bhp at 7600 rpm while the power output of the Mondial 8 is 214 bhp at 7500 rpm.

The 512 S was agressive, even brutal looking, but for all that the total package added up to a sleek, low slung racing car in either berlinetta or spider form. The elegantly formed body from nose to tail was fabricated in reinforced fibre-glass by Cigarla and Bertinetti, the moulds being taken from 'masters' formed at the works.

Three cars were expected to take to the circuits for the main championship events in 1970, and of the remaining 22 cars being built some were to be sold to other teams, privateers and some retained at the factory as replacements and for spares. Homologation by the F.I.A. had been delayed due to labour problems at the works but most of the required 25 cars had been built and the remainder were in the final stages of completion. One problem remained, however, when the F.I.A. refused to accept the roll bar structure. Ferrari refused to make any changes and informed the authorities that his cars would not race if he was forced to comply with their request. The F.I.A. capitulated, as they had on a number of previous occasions when Ferrari had been adamant.

During its short life as a works car, the 512 S was to be seen in five

changes had reduced the overall weight by nearly 40 kilos. For the important Le Mans 24 hour race a long tail (coda lunga) was fitted. The spider model followed the general lines of the berlinetta (obviously without a closed in driving compartment) but had a foreshortened tail exposing the rear end, and the louvred engine cover had been dispensed with.

The 512 M (M for modificata) series was first seen at the final round of the championship with revised aerodynamic bodywork. It was a berlinetta with a carburettor airscoop located at the rear of the cockpit roof, the tail line less of a protrusion with two small adjustable wings. Further work had been carried out on the suspension and engine. The 512 M was not a new model and 10 of the 'S' cars which had been sold and which were returned to the factory by their owners were 'converted' to 'M' specification. A further four were converted by their owners using works parts and one had been rebuilt as a spider, but at a later date this car reverted to the original berlinetta bodywork.

Neither the 512 S nor the 512 M distinguished themselves on the

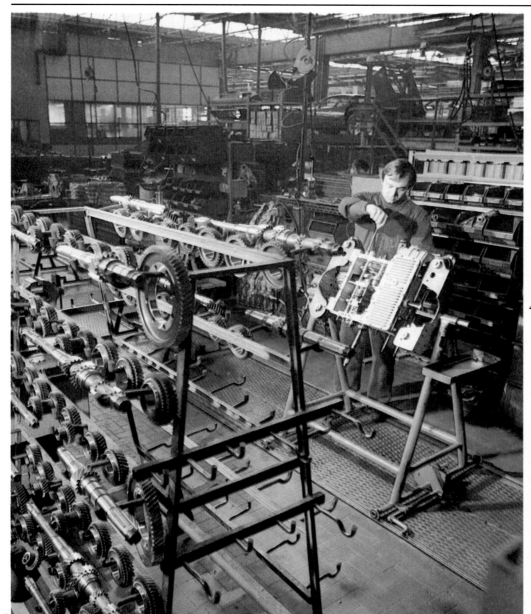

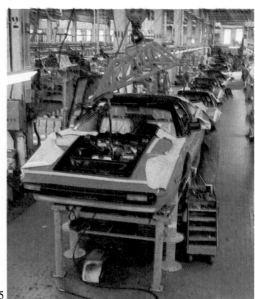

(3) Assembly of the gearboxes for the V8 engines. Both the 308 series and Mondial 8 have 5-speed all synchromesh and reverse gears. (4) The drill-mill as seen at work on a V8 gearbox. (5) Assembly line for the 308 series. Much work is still to be done before the cars roll out of the factory.

circuits although they participated in a championship which had, up to that time (1970/1971), promised to be the most exciting period of sports racing, with the Ferraris having a top speed of around 218 mph against their opponents, the Porsche 917s, with a reputed speed of about 240 mph. It was the old story repeating itself, as a new formula for the Championship of Makes for Group 6 cars was on the way, and Ferrari was concentrating on the 312 PB, which would run with the well tried formula 1 engine but in a detuned version, as race distances were longer. So once more diversification had allowed what should have been a promising concept to founder. A great shame as it was, and still is, a great car.

The 512 S made its debut at Daytona in the 24 hour race on January 31st 1970. Five berlinettas were entered, three by the works, one by N.A.R.T. and one from Scuderia Picchio Rosso. The Andretti/Merzario/Ickx factory car finished 3rd behind two Porsches, the N.A.R.T. car failed to finish and the other three were involved in accidents. The 12 hour race at Sebring followed on March 21st with a berlinetta and two spiders from the works and another spider from N.A.R.T. Fortune smiled on this occasion as the Vaccerella/Giunti/ Andretti berlinetta took the chequered flag but N.A.R.T's spider had an accident and the other works' spiders failed to finish.

So the 1970 season progressed, with factory cars, other team cars, and privateers competing in no less than 21 events in Europe, the Americas, South Africa and Japan, Scuderia Ferrari participating in 13 of these. In all there were 62 entries of 512 cars in these events, and apart from 11 cars involved in accidents only 15 entrants failed to finish a race, which would indicate that reliability was a strong point.

Although the factory 512 S cars did not have the successes hoped for, some good performances were recorded in the championship, that is apart from the complete fiasco at the prestigious annual Le Mans 24 hour race on June 14, when 10 berlinettas (including 4 works cars) and one spider were entered. Rain fell during the early part of the race and Reine Wisell, who was sharing a Filipinetti team berlinetta with Bonnier, slowed down owing to oil on his windscreen which had cut his visibility. Coming up fast Regazzoni, in a works car, hit him and Parkes, driving another Filipinetti team berlinetta, and in the confusion Derek Bell overturned his works 512 S, resulting in four Ferraris being eliminated at one go. Later the Giunti/Vaccarella factory car had engine trouble and the Gelo (G. Loos racing) team of Loos/Kellners retired with a badly damaged nose, while the Moretti/Manfredini 512 S entered jointly by the factory and Scuderia Picchio Rosso retired to the 'dead car' park

with a dry gearbox. After nine hours, while in third place, the Ickx/Schetty car had a rear brake lock, sending Ickx off the circuit and killing a marshal, the car then burst into flames and was partly destroyed. Next to go was the Juncadell/Fernandez spider, out with a split gearbox casing. However, three Ferraris finished the race; the N.A.R.T. berlinetta entry driven by Posey/Bucknum which finished fourth and the Ecurie Francorchamps berlinetta driven by Walker/de Fierland in fifth place. A lone 312 P Ferrari was unplaced as it had not covered a great enough distance.

It was after the Le Mans debacle that Ferrari, always a battler, modified and developed further the 'S' model, one of which was ready to run at Zeltweg for the Austrian 1000 km on October 11th.

However, the 512 S factory cars had three further outings before the

(1 & 2) The front-engined 4.4 litre V12 twin overhead camshaft per bank of cylinders 365GTB/4 (commonly called the Daytona), could be considered as the last V12 road car designed by Enzo Ferrari and was in production for five years from 1968. Whilst it is not one of Pininfarina's more classic coachwork styles, the lines have, over the years, become appreciated by Ferrarists and even in the current financial climate the model maintains a high selling price in the used car market. A Spider version was also available from 1971 and such models command a much higher price; so much so that many owners of the berlinetta had them converted to Spiders. It is only by knowing the chassis numbers of the factory built spiders that the 'conversions' can be separated from the originals. (3) The engine compartment of the Daytona.

4

KPE 650W

5

GPG 747V

6

512 M appeared. Two spiders contested the Watkins Glen 6 hour race on July 11, when Andretti/Giunti made third place and Ickx/Schetty were placed fifth. The same cars (chassis numbers 1042 and 1010) appeared the following day, also at Watkins Glen, for the Can Am event when Andretti placed his spider fifth but Ickx failed to finish.

The 512 M sent to Zeltweg was the same car (chassis number 1010) which Ickx had driven at Watkins Glen in July, and apart from the engine and other modifications, it had been converted from a spider into the new style berlinetta bodywork. The new car, with Ickx at the wheel, was extremely fast and had the legs of the Porches early in the race, setting up a new record for the circuit, but unfortunately electrical problems caused its retirement. The 512 M was then 'shipped' out to South Africa for the Kyalami 9 hour event, where it started from pole position, and the Ickx/Giunti driver combination stayed in front to take the chequered flag. Ecurie Francorchamps had joined the works car with their 512 S, but Derek Bell and de Fierland could finish no higher than sixth.

The last time the factory raced the 512 M was at Imola on May 2nd 1971 for a 300 km race when Merzario took the berlinetta, with chassis number 1010, to victory.

1971 was not the year of the 512 M. The cars had been sold off to a variety of teams and individuals who competed not only in the championship events, receiving assistance from the factory, but also in a number of other races, some of importance. Apart from Merzario's win at Imola, the only other first place was at the Ecuador 12 hour event when Young, driving a spider version of the 512 M, took the chequered flag.

The best known and without doubt the fastest 512 M belonged to the Penske/White organisation and was driven by Mark Donohue and David Hobbs in long distance races, but that little bit of luck was never on their side.

Other well known teams who bought and raced the 512s, apart from those already mentioned, were Herbert Muller Racing, Scuderia Brescia/Corse, Escuderia Montjuich, and Earl-Cord Racing.

With a few exceptions the racing careers of the 512 Ms finished at the close of the 1971 season. However, they may be seen even today, racing in suitable events in the USA and the United Kingdom, having been fully restored by their present owners. It is interesting to note that the 512 M owned by Robert Horne still holds two British records achieved on the main runway at Fairford aerodrome in 1977 despite poor weather conditions. In Class C, Derek Bell holds the flying start 500 metre record at 187.34 mph and Robert Horne the 1 mile flying start record at 191.64 mph.

The 512 S and M V12 cars should and no doubt would have recorded many wins if only the factory had not 'abandoned' the design before their full development. An opportunity lost?

(4 & 6) Both photographs show the exquisite shape of one of the most popular 'lines' to have come from the factory: the 308 series. The top picture is of the Spider model but with the detachable roof still in place, whilst the bottom head-on view shows why Ferraris are show-stoppers.

The front spoiler adds to the overall near perfect flowing symmetry, which is the hallmark of the craftsmen at Pininfarina. (5) The lines of the 512BB are similar to those of the 308s but the front view gives an impression of brute strength rather than elegance. Note the 'pop-up' headlamps.

ROAD-CAR TAKEOVER BY FIAT

Predicting the future should be left to the soothsayers, astrologers and the compilers of Old Moore's Almanac, and if they have their problems in getting it right, (which they do), the chances of trying to probe the minds of marketing men, designers and engineers in the automobile industry is fraught with many pitfalls. It could be said that in these times, certain guidelines have been established in both engine and body design based on the need to conserve the world's dwindling energy resources. But while a large section of the motoring population is concerned solely with a means of trouble free transportation, and therefore do not take

1

2

3

4

*(1, 2 & 3) The 308GT4 2 + 2 made its
appearance at the Paris Show in 1973 and
remained in production for seven years
until it was superseded by the Mondial 8,
which is also a 2 + 2 car. The mechanics of
the 308GT4 are similar to those of the
308GTB/GTS but the coachwork was
designed by Bertone and executed, as in
most cases, by Scaglietti. For the first three
years of its production it wore the Dino
badge but was then given the Ferrari logo.
Not one of the most handsome of Ferraris,
but it should be borne in mind that with
four seats it is always difficult for a
designer to get a flowing line, and
Bertone's compromise grows on the
beholder. A first class roadholder, the
308GT4 is now coming into 'fashion' with
good used examples more than holding
their market value.*

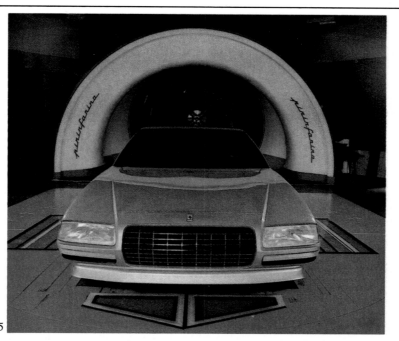

5

*(4, 5 & 6) The Ferrari Pinin has been on
the 'stocks' for some two years and will
probably be marketed in 1983. This is the
first four door saloon ever produced
bearing the illustrious Ferrari name and
badge. Whilst the purist will in all
probability not acknowledge it as coming
from the same stable as its predecessors,
FIAT required an up-market car and in
this instance it challenges the Rolls-Royce,
being a high speed comfortable four-seater
limousine. The 5-litre flat 12 boxer
engine is mounted at the front and the
driver has a mass of computerised
instruments on the fascia on which he
needs to keep his eyes! There can be no
doubt that whilst the lines are hardly
Ferrari, it is a handsome automobile with
a very striking frontal aspect.*

6

into account design factors, there are still those who are more discerning, preferring the exotic to the mundane, and as long as a free market exists there will always be a multitude of engine designs and body shapes from which to choose.

The whole concept of a Ferrari might have been changed during the sixties, when the Ford Motor Company in America decided it might have something to gain by becoming actively involved in European motor racing, thinking no doubt that any publicity from possible successes would benefit the sales of their passenger cars. So it was that, after the 1963 Le Mans 24 hour endurance race, when Ferraris had notched up their seventh win, Fords supposedly made an approach to Enzo Ferrari hoping to persuade him to sell out. Such a move would have given the company a ready made base and organisation from which it could operate in Europe. On the other hand it was rumoured

that Ferrari had made the initial move, but such points are now academic as the talks were called off.

What Ford's would have done with Ferrari can only be conjecture. Would they have retained only the racing department and sold off that part of the works dealing with the road cars, or if they had retained the road cars organisation would these have been Americanised, in which case the Italian flair for designing and building exotic cars would have been lost? Perhaps it was as well that Ferrari pulled back!

More significant, however, was FIAT'S take-over of the Ferrari road car business in late 1969. Outwardly nothing seemed to change during the first 10 to 11 years, but this was not unexpected since the incubation period for a new car is a lengthy process, particularly in a large organisation where accountants, marketing men, technicians, engineers and others all have a hand in the final product. During this period the FIAT

1

(1 & 5) At the 1980 Geneva Show the Mondial 8 2 + 2 was unveiled, signalling the demise of its predecessor, the 308GT4, which was also a 2 + 2. However, the design for the new 2 + 2 was entrusted to Pininfarina, who perhaps made a rather better job of styling the car than Bertone's effort on the 308GT4. The wheelbase of the new 2 + 2 had been extended by 4 inches, which was an advantage, and the overall height had also been increased so that passenger comfort for four people was not so restrictive. Perhaps the one blemish in the styling are the engine air intakes which look a bit gimmicky. Had the scoop been taken further forward into the door panelling (as for the 308 series), the overall side view would have given a 'softer' and more flowing line. Bosch K-Jetronic fuel

2

3

injection has replaced the Weber carburettors to give a smoother drive. Suspension at both the front and rear is fully independent and air-conditioning for the passengers is a standard and not extra feature. While the motive power follows that of the 308 series it is detuned to the extent that the output is some 41 bhp down on its 'sister' cars. The Mondial 8 can be considered, with the 400 series, as being FIAT inspired. *(2, 3, 4 & 6) Different views of the new fuel injection 308GTBi and GTSi current models.*

company and other industries in Italy were having a hard time, especially in 1974 when strikes were widespread and unions were making unreasonable demands. In fact FIAT had a quarter of a million unsold cars and no markets. So during the early years of the FIAT take-over of the road cars, Ferraris which had been on the drawing boards some years earlier and which showed their race breeding, continued to be manufactured. Such cars as the V12 front engined Daytona berlinetta and spider (365 GTB/4 and 365 GTS/4), the Dino 246 GT and spider version 246 GTS (the 2.4 litre V6 engine which was produced in the FIAT factory also powered the highly successful Lancia Stratos Rally cars), the 365/BB to be followed by the BB 512, both with the Boxer flat 12 cylinder unit, and finally the 308 series first as a 2+2 car (four seats) then as a berlinetta and finally as a spider. The BB 512, 308 GTB and GTS now have fuel injection and the 308 GT4 2+2 has been phased out and replaced by the Mondial 8, which is also a 2+2 car and undoubtedly a FIAT Ferrari. Of the foregoing cars only the Daytona had an engine at the front, the remainder having the unit placed behind the driving compartment.

Perhaps the first sign of FIAT influence was the 400 GT with either manual or automatic transmission. Relying on the familiar V12 Ferrari engine at the front, it is a full four seater with all the necessary comforts and speed for gran turismo travel. Neither Ferrari nor FIAT, up to 1976 when the 400 GT was first shown, at the Paris Salon, had a car to challenge the growing 'up-market' demand for an executive automobile. The Aston Martin, Jaguar (including the Daimler), Mercedes, Maserati and BMW, in Europe, had been making inroads into this market, and although the 400 GT cost rather more than these, an executive car with the prancing horse insignia had greater prestige and it could and did capture some of the exclusive Rolls Royce market.

In the more sporting but still high price market Ferrari, with the 308 series, has never been seriously challenged by such makes as the Porsche in its various forms, or even the Lotus, but the berlinetta is now seven years old and the spider five. Both have recently been modified using the Bosch K Jetronic fuel injection system, but it seems likely that the car will be replaced in the near future.

4

5

6

1

2

At the top end of the market, excluding the Rolls Royce which does not compete in this bracket, is the 512 BBi which is also fuel injected. The only other car in the same market is the Lamborghini Countach, but such cars are rare and do not pose any threat to the Ferrari. Having said that, it is difficult to see where cars of this calibre fit into the general scheme of any manufacturer in the future and perhaps these two are the last of a dying breed—the supercars. More's the pity, for in a grey world where governments seem to strive for uniformity, the glamour and excitement of the supercars adds a little more zest to life, whether they are affordable or not.

A little earlier in this chapter it was stated that the Mondial 8 was undoubtedly a FIAT Ferrari, and perhaps an observation such as this should be substantiated. This model or tipo is the first Ferrari to be planned, designed and built under FIAT direction. Seemingly there is little to differentiate the Mondial 8 from its sister the 308 GTBi. The former uses the basic suspension components and general running gear of the latter and both have the same 90° V8 transverse mid-engine, with a bore of 81 mm and a stroke of 71 mm giving a capacity of 2926 cc. There are also twin overhead camshafts per bank of cylinders and Bosch K-Jetronic fuel injection. From here on the Mondial 8 differs substantially from the 308 GTBi. The wheelbase has been increased by 12 inches making it 104 inches against the 308 GTBi wheelbase of 92 inches and the overall length is 13.8″ greater. More importantly, which detracts from the aesthetic appeal, the overall height has been raised five inches, giving the rear passengers more headroom than was found in the 308 GT4 2+2 which it replaced, and with body width increased by three

(1, 2, 3, 4 & 5) The factory had never really built a limousine type car as the previous gran turismo models had always been based on designs with racing connections. The 400GT could be had with either a manual or automatic gearbox. A Pininfarina designed and built car, the engine is a front-mounted 5-litre V12. Originally, in 1976, there were 6 Weber carburettors but these were replaced in 1979 by fuel injection. There is power steering and, of course, air-conditioning.

inches, the interior is naturally more roomy. Although these extra inches may seem minimal, they give the whole of the driving and rear seating compartment an illusion of even greater space when the extra headroom is taken into consideration.

Other refinements are; greater driver leg-room and all the requirements considered necessary for today's exotic cars to ensure that the driver is fully aware of what is happening at all times when he is at the wheel. No doubt of great appeal to many is the additional room for luggage, in fact it is almost up to the capacity of many other manufacturers' cars who make great play of the storage room!

Although the styling is by Pininfarina, arguably the best coach designer in the world, the Mondial 8 lacks that essential Ferrari aesthetic look. It should be remembered however, that to get 'that' look with a 2+2 is no easy matter, especially if it is intended that the rear seats are to be used by adults, and not by midgets or simply for stowing away extra baggage or shopping. Perhaps the total package is spoiled by the rear air-scoop grilles, and here it would seem as though Pininfarina was trying to imitate similar ducts which he had 'built into' a show design designated 250 P5, first displayed at Geneva in 1968, but in this instance the scoop was carried forward into the doors, as in the 308 series, which would have made the design more acceptable. To round off the whole, the bumpers are wrap-around giving useful all round protection.

The Mondial 8 is obviously the first in a line of automobiles which heralds the complete take over of Ferrari road-cars by FIAT. Cars which are built to be used and not just to be seen in, although a car with the 1

Called by some the flagship of the Ferrari fleet, by others Ferrari's Macho Missile but perhaps regarded by all as the last of the Supercars. While it may earn all these titles, like all cars, the 512BBi has its faults, for there is no manufacturer who can build perfection into any machinery. The model was first seen by the public at the 1976 Paris Show and while there have been modifications over the years, the horizontally opposed 12-cylinder engine received an extended life when the 4 triple choke down draught Weber carburettors were replaced in 1982 with the Bosch K-Jetronic injection system. The engine has a bore/stroke of 82 mm/78 mm giving a capacity of 4943 cc and lies longitudinally, and not transversely, behind the driver. Unusually, it is mounted above the 5-speed and reverse gearbox. There are, of course, twin overhead camshafts per bank of cylinders, and the maximum power output is 340 bhp at 6000 rpm.
The 512BBi is hardly in keeping with grand touring as the amount of space available for baggage is minimal.

prancing horse motif will always, it is hoped, be a 'crowd-stopper'.

The next FIAT to be marketed will in all probability be what is at present known as the 'Pinin'. First shown some two years ago, the car is aimed at the top-bracket executive, and if looks are any criterion it should be chauffeur driven; something which any true Ferrarist could never contemplate. The line, in general, follows that of the 400 series although more curvaceous, but the rear seated passengers will not be inconvenienced by having to scramble through the front doors since it is a four door limousine of true elegance and sumptuous comfort. It should be marketed in 1983 with the 5 litre flat-12 boxer engine mounted at the front.

Time moves on, and the car a true Ferrarist wants is not in sight, although rumour has it that the ultimate berlinetta boxer is still to come, 3

4

so maybe the day of the supercar is not yet over.

So what of the future? It is essential that any design has to be a model for daily use under all types of conditions, but it should on the other hand be a Ferrari, which means a trend-setter and not a car marketed to compete with the BMWs, Mercedes, Maseratis, Jaguars, and their like. A Ferrari, like a true Ferrarist, means a special breed of car and man or woman. Economics and energy resources play no part as there is, and will be, sufficient cash and fuel available for the foreseeable future, which means a market for a car for the specialist.

The 'form' of the car would always be argued over by the Ferrarist, most of whom have their own strongly held ideals, even if these have some minor imperfections. To most Ferrarists the engine would be a front-mounted V12 with 3 valves and 2 plugs per cylinder, with twin overhead camshafts per bank of cylinders and fuel injection. Transmission would also be front mounted five speed syncromesh and reverse. Suspension all independent. Air conditioning and instrumen-

tation etc. to conform to modern specification.

Perhaps the most difficult decision to make would be the styling, but Pininfarina designs from the mid-sixties would not be outdated in the eighties, in fact a number would bring a refreshing change to the 'look-alike' cars of today.

Since the car is road-going, a number of sports and GT racing designs should be ignored. This being so there can surely be no more handsome, curvaceous and voluptuous looking Ferrari than the 275 GTB designed by Pininfarina, with the 'power-bulge' on the bonnet and the quarterlights removed to ensure continuity of a smooth line. This car, seen at a number of motor shows in 1965 would even today be a crowd puller.

However, it is doubtful whether the marketing men would have the clock put back, although they just might decide to follow the lead of Porsche, who have abandoned rear-engines, deciding that the future lies with the power unit under the front bonnet.

REVIVAL OF THE GTO

Ferrari genius, Scaglietti skill and Pininfarina flair combined yet again to produce, in 1984, an outstanding masterpiece – the beautiful GTO (left). Originally limited to a run of just 200 examples, production eventually exceeded this figure by 71.

Below: chic red and black seating continues the sporting theme in the GTO's interior. Originally designed as a competition car, all production models wore red livery, and came fully equipped with air conditioning and stereo system.

Every year is a special year for Ferrari, but 1984 saw the relaunch of perhaps the most famous model name in Ferrari history: the GTO.

Twenty-three years earlier Ferrari had launched their original GTO (Gran Turismo Omologato), which had been produced to get round the FIA motor sport rules, and today this is perhaps the most valuable of all Ferrari models.

The announcement of the new GTO at the 1984 Geneva Motor Show could have been seen as a marketing exercise, but when the specification was released it was clear that this was no ordinary Ferrari. Codenamed the Ferrari 288 GTO, it had a V8 engine of 2,855cc and twin turbochargers producing 400 bhp. Ferrari had used turbocharging in their Grand Prix cars since 1981, but in the GTO they used twin turbochargers from IHI of Japan rather than the KKK turbos of the Grand Prix cars. The GTO became the fastest road-going Ferrari built to that time, and the first to exceed 300 kph (186 mph).

The car followed the 308 design principles with a central tubular frame, but the wheelbase was lengthened due to the rearrangement of the engine and turbochargers. Clearly this was a high performance car which was likely to be in great demand, and costly to boot. As though to add to the car's appeal, Ferrari announced that only 200 examples would be produced and that these would be shared out on the world market pro-rata to the number of Ferrari cars sold in that market the previous year. As is often the case, however, the true number of 288 GTO's built exceeded this figure by 71, with more than half of them going, not-unnaturally, to the United States. All were finished in Ferrari red with black upholstery, and all were quickly snapped up.

Equipped with twin IHI turbos and Behr intercoolers, the 228 GTO's 2855 cc V8 engine (above) propelled the car to a top speed of 190 mph, making this the fastest road-going Ferrari at the time of its launch.

Facing page: the original GTO, the 250 of 1962. Built by Scaglietti, most of the GTOs used 3-litre V8 engines, but a handful made use of the 4-litre unit from the Superamerica. Only 39 examples were built.

Above: a detail shot of the Testarossa's alloy wheels reveals the Ferrari stamp of quality.

Below: more than mere decoration, the slats on the Testarossa's sides channel air into the engine's twin radiators.

Looking predatory even from the rear, this fabulous Testarossa (above) of 1986 bears little resemblance to its illustrious racing predecessor of the Fifties.

Left: a detail of the huge air vents that stretch along almost the full length of the doors.

Facing page top: seen in profile, the Testarossa shows its Latin breeding. Styled by Pininfarina, the design is a triumphant fusion of aesthetics and aerodynamics.

Below: a development of the Berlinetta Boxer unit, the Testarossa's huge 5-litre flat 12 engine features four valves per cylinder and Bosch K-Jetronic fuel injection. All this punch is transferred to the wheels via a twin-disc clutch and five-speed transaxle manual transmission.

Facing page bottom: variously referred to as slats or egg slicer, the Testarossa vents were necessary because of the location of radiators at the back of the car rather than in the front, as on the related Berlinetta Boxer.

Below: with a top speed of some 180 mph, calibration on the Testarossa's speedometer is no idle boast.

Not content with the sensational impact of the GTO, Ferrari followed it up at the 1984 Paris Show with the Ferrari Testarossa, the replacement to the successful Berlinetta Boxer. In its various forms, the Boxer had been in production for twelve years and the new car with its low and squat profile was to prove just as sensational and desirable as the BB had been. The styling was created by Pininfarina, with the main emphasis being on producing a car which had both aesthetic appeal and an aerodynamic shape. The Testarossa – a named after the sports racing car of the mid Fifties with its red, crackle painted camshaft covers – was an instant success, and like the GTO a few months earlier, led to a queue of customers with money at the ready.

Meanwhile, the original Mondial 3-litre, introduced in August 1981, had been replaced a year later by the Mondial Quattro Valvole, but it too was to be replaced in 1982 by the 3.2-litre version which remained unchanged until late 1989, when it was completely facelifted.

During 1985, Ferrari made a number of technical changes to their cars, many of twhich were now being challenged by other makes, notably Porsche, Mercedes and BMW, all of whom were targetting cars for what could be called the Ferrari niche market.

During the year some old friends were replaced. The 308GTB and GTB/I, introduced in 1976, and the 308 four valve (Quattrovalvole) were dropped in August 1985 and replaced by the 328 GTB and the 308 GTS respectively. Meanwhile, the big Pininfarina-bodied 400 was given a 340 bhp 5-litre V12 engine and renamed the 412. It was available either in automatic or manual form for the same price.

For those who thought that the performance bubble had burst and that the day of the supercar had come to an end, a surprise was in store. The doubters, however, failed to interpret and understand the ethos and pride of Maranello who, faced with such challengers as Porsche with the 959 and the continuing, if weak, role of Lamborghini, were not about to cast off the charisma of sheer power and pace.

To celebrate 40 years in the motor industry, something very special was needed and though he was now becoming very old and frail and, indeed, had never been a true convert to the production of road cars rather than his beloved racing cars, the distinctive touch of Enzo Ferrari could still be seen behind the thinking which produced quite the most remarkable two-seater GT. Indeed, it is difficult to imagine that the Nineties will see anything to match the sheer panache and excess of the Ferrari F40.

Cars such as the GTO, Daytona, BB and the Testarossa almost paled into insignificance when faced with this squat, functional car with its high tail wing. Although slotted into the Grand Touring category by the marketing men, it was and is a pure racing car mildly tamed for the road. Although capable of being driven relatively smoothly by a competent driver, in the hands of a skilled racing driver it could deliver the kind of performance and handling that one only finds in the higher echelons of the World Sports Car Championship.

The F40 is remarkably small and compact, the engine compartment, reached by an upward-hinging tailgate, jam packed with the centrally mounted four-valve 3-litre turbocharged V8 Ferrari. Producing 478 bhp with this package, the car has a top speed of 200 mph and can reach 125 mph from a standing start in just 12 seconds!

In complete contrast to the F40, Ferrari quietly announced the 498 project, a small four-wheel drive saloon with electronic suspension, and one that was seemingly totally out of character with past Ferrari policy. In the late 1950s, however, Enzo Ferrari had worked on a small 850 cc four-cylinder engine with a view to producing a small saloon. With the arrival of Fiat, however, the whole 854 project was sold off to a private company and became the ASA Mille.

The latest in a long line of Ferrari
supercars, the superlative F40 (below
and right) celebrated forty years of
Ferrari car manufacture. Modena's
answer to the Porsche 959, this wolf in
wolf's clothing screams to 60 mph from
a standing start in a breath-stopping 3
seconds, and keeps pulling to a fraction
over 200 mph. Largely based on the
GTO, the car took just twelve months
to develop.

Above: a sleek, elegant coupé, this
1988 412 is far from most people's idea
of a Ferrari. Powered by a 5-litre V12
engine, this exclusive Grand Tourer
was capable of a top speed in the region
of 150 mph.

Left: the flowing lines of a 1988
Ferrari 328 GTB. Built by Scaglietti
to a Pininfarina design, this model is a
development of the 308, having a larger
version of the latter's V8 engine. Also
available as an open top, designated the
GTS, the 328 was one of the most
successful models to have been produced
by Ferrari.

So what are the portents of the 498? A move into the high performance small saloon market with the cachet of the Ferrari name? Time alone will tell.

In 1986 Ferrari continued their steady development programme by launching the 208 Turbo, which was available in the familiar GTB, closed, and GTS, Targa-top, forms. As the numbering system would indicate, it was a 2-litre V8 with fuel infection and turbocharging. Turbocharged engines were very much in vogue in the mid-1980s, although their popularity was to wane somewhat as the decade came to an end and multivalve engines became more attractive. The 208 Turbo produced 254 bhp, which gave it a maximum speed of nearly 160 mph. As with other Dino models, the 208 was not over-endowed with luggage room, and although built as a superb Grand Touring car the capacity of 8.6 cubic feet did not measure up to that associated with touring models.

The death of Enzo Ferrari in 1988 brought to an end the classic era of Ferrari. Any thoughts that this factor would bring Fiat into more direct control of the company were clearly inappropriate as Fiat had long since taken over full control of the development and manufacturing of the production cars. If Ferrari's death meant one thing it could be that it would give the green light for Ferrari to look more closely at the luxury four-door saloon market – an area in which Enzo Ferrari had no interest.

A year later, in 1989, far from seeing a dip in sales due to the death of its founder, Ferrari found themselves in a healthier position than ever. The new President of Ferrari was Piero Fusaro, and in the 1989 trading year Ferrari profits rose by an impressive 36 percent. At the same time Ferrari's once-dominant and position at the top of the dream car league was being challenged by a host of cars which offered similar performance. To counter the threat, Fiat increased the Ferrari's research and development budget. Far from being weaker, Ferrari were now stronger.

The car that dreams are made of is itself made of weight-saving Kevlar, carbon fibre and fibreglass over a steel tube chassis. Despite the astronomical prices being quoted for the few F40s that are likely to be built, this is not a luxury car, neither is it as well specified mechanically as the Porsche, lacking the latter's sophisticated suspension, four-wheel drive and braking system. For all its apparent limitations, however, this red-blooded racer produces results and will, in fact, edge past the Stuttgart machine in the speed and acceleration stakes and is one of the most exciting Ferraris of all time.

Above: with doors open and hood and engine covers raised, the F40 loses its characteristic good looks. Beneath the Scaglietti-built body lurks a twin-turbo 3-litre V8 engine that develops 470 bhp at 7,000 rpm. With alternative turbo packages output can be boosted by an unbelievable 200 bhp!

During that year we saw the latest development on familiar themes, with the 328 GTB giving way to the 348T. The 348 was clearly going in a different direction, its 3.4-litre version of the 32-valve V8 giving it an additional 30 bhp as well as a lift in torque. The car was completely redesigned, with a wedge-shaped body smoothed off at the front and Testarossa style air slots on the side panels, ABS brakes, Bosch Motronic ignition and a transverse gearbox.

The 1990 world economic downturn saw the Ferrari market take a knock, but the effects of the recession were felt by other car makers as well.

If we are to look for pointers to the future then we must look around us. Pininfarina appeared at the Tokyo Motor Show with the Mythos, a striking open sports car using the Testarossa floor pan and mechanicals. With wide, sweeping lines it was a dramatic car in many respects, boasting an adjustable rear spoiler and many other interesting aerodynamic and styling touches. It is not the first time that Ferrari and Pininfarina have combined to produce a show car that points the way forward, and even though this style of open car may never be built, some of the detail work is likely to see its way into production. Whatever the future holds in terms of new models, what is certain is that the Ferrari name will continue to delight all who share a passion for exotic automobiles.